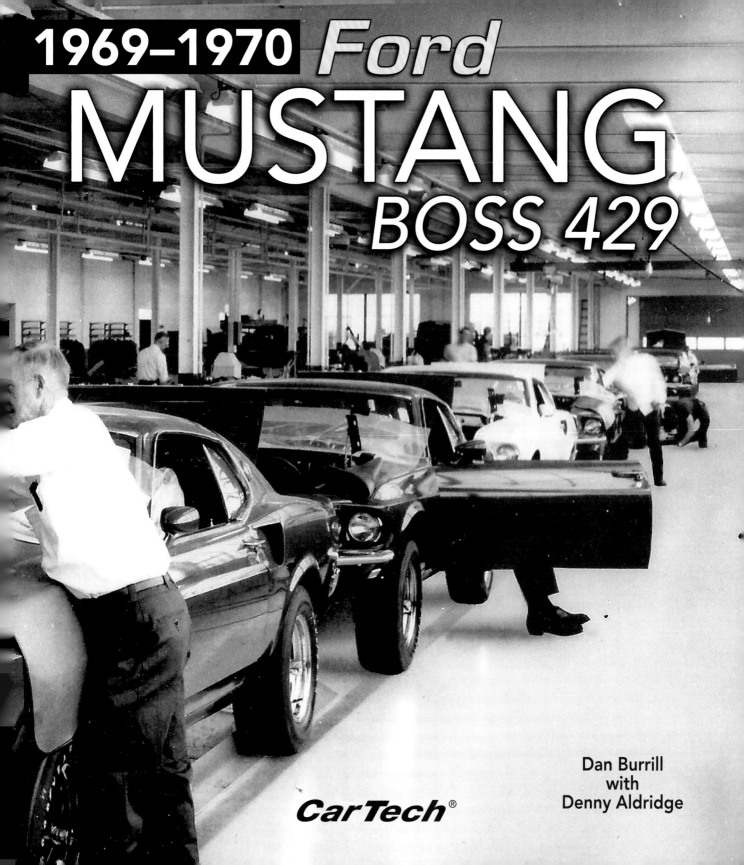

1969–1970 *Ford*
MUSTANG
BOSS 429

Dan Burrill
with
Denny Aldridge

CarTech®

CarTech®

CarTech®, Inc.
838 Lake Street South
Forest Lake, MN 55025
Phone: 651-277-1200 or 800-551-4754
Fax: 651-277-1203
www.cartechbooks.com

Edit by Paul Johnson
Layout by Monica Seiberlich

ISBN 978-1-61325-316-8
Item No. CT587

Library of Congress Cataloging-in-Publication Data Available

Written, edited, and designed in the U.S.A.
Printed in China
10 9 8 7 6 5 4 3 2 1

Title Page:
The engineers and assembly workers at Kar-Kraft are assembling automotive history as these 1969 Boss 429s receive the mammoth big-block engine. It took a team of at least four people to fit the engine into place. Two were above and two were below. (Photo Courtesy Ford Images)

Frontispiece:
The Boss 429 is a formidable engine, and it was a tight squeeze into the Mustang. It is shown here with an aftermarket air cleaner. The engine draws more air than the factory snorkel does and factory air cleaners are very expensive to replace if they are stolen or damaged. Rated at 375 hp, these engines often produce 480 to 520 hp on the dyno. Race-engine horsepower can be pumped up to 1,100 or 1,200.

Contents Page:
This is KK 1737. It has never been restored and has only 15,000 miles on the odometer. It has been part of the Aldridge collection for more than 35 years. It is currently on display at the World of Speed Museum in Wilsonville, Oregon.

DISTRIBUTION BY:

Europe
PGUK
63 Hatton Garden
London EC1N 8LE, England
Phone: 020 7061 1980 • Fax: 020 7242 3725
www.pguk.co.uk

Australia
Renniks Publications Ltd.
3/37-39 Green Street
Banksmeadow, NSW 2109, Australia
Phone: 2 9695 7055 • Fax: 2 9695 7355
www.renniks.com

Canada
Login Canada
300 Saulteaux Crescent
Winnipeg, MB, R3J-3T2, Canada
Phone: 800-665-1148 • Fax: 800-665-0103
www.LB.ca

TABLE OF CONTENTS

429.222 Bur

DEDICATION

To Pam Aldridge, for all her help and support in this year-long project. It would have been difficult to complete this project without you.

ACKNOWLEDGMENTS

Writing a book of this nature is not something that can be done without the help of many people who are willing to share their stories, photos, recollections, and memorabilia. Only a few people have made it their business to become experts on the Boss 429; one of those is Denny Aldridge, owner of Aldridge Motorsports and Engineering. Currently, he has in his collection 1 1969 Boss 302 and 4 1969 Boss 429 Mustangs. Over the years, he has owned 37 Boss 302 Mustangs and 15 Boss 429 Mustangs. His company has been a Ford Racing dealer for the past 32 years and a Roush Racing dealer since 1972.

I was fortunate that Denny was willing to share his vast knowledge, expertise, and archives with me. Without his generous help, this book would not have been possible.

I am grateful to a very special and dedicated group of people for generously sharing their knowledge and photographs, as well as making available all of the unusual racing parts necessary to complete this book: Len Ewell, for his help in researching historical and technical information and for sharing his extensive library of reference materials; Randy Hernandez supplied his dad's rare photos and memorabilia, which was a great help in filling in the blanks for the Kar-Kraft operation; and Sig Hustad, Dan Spiegel, and Richard Truesdell for supplying their excellent photos. Doing research for this book required the better part of a year. I used other sources, of course, and it would have been impossible to have an accurate project without their help. I also want to thank Joe Spinelli for reviewing the manuscript and offering his advice and expert knowledge of these very special cars.

Last, but absolutely not least, I wish to thank my editor, Paul Johnson, for giving me the opportunity, his insightful advice, and his hard work in turning the rough draft into a finished manuscript.

The 1970 Boss 429 Mustang featured new body styling. The front end had only two headlights and the front fenders had decorative air vents, whereas the older 1969 body style featured two additional headlights. Today, the 1969 cars are considered to be the more desirable of the two.

The seeds for creation of the Boss 429 were planted in 1964. That year, Chrysler brought the 426 Hemi to Daytona where it cleaned up in Daytona 500 qualifiers and the race. Ford realized that the race version of the FE 427, with its cam-in-block and pushrod setup, could not surpass Mopar's elephant engine. The Blue Oval's solution to the problem was to install the 427 SOHC (single overhead cam engine), otherwise known as the Cammer 427, in Ford and Mercury stock cars. In January 1964, Ford requested NASCAR's approval to use the Cammer engine for competition, but Bill France turned them down.

Ford needed its own version of the Hemi. After NASCAR effectively rejected the Cammer, Ford began the design and development of the engine that became known as the Boss 429. After the long, anguishing saga of trying to homologate the FE 427 Cammer for NASCAR racing, Henry Ford II and Ford racing personnel were determined to build an engine that would fit into the NASCAR rulebooks. The goal was to beat the Hemi and all other big-block challengers in NASCAR competition, as well as at quarter-mile drag strips across the country. From the beginning, the Boss 429 was a limited-build race homologation street car, built to conform to NASCAR rules. It became one of the most valuable and rare Mustangs ever built.

Ford already had the very successful FE Series 427, followed by the 428 and 428 Cobra Jet, so why the Boss 429? It boiled down to Bill France Sr., the owner and general manager of NASCAR. He owned the tracks

7

and he made the rules. Smokey Yunick once referred to him as a dictator and stated that he "made up the rules as he went along." Keep in mind that in the 1960s, success in NASCAR was an important part of the racing program. The automobile manufacturers desperately wanted their cars on the tracks, exposed to the media and the public, especially the Daytona 500. This was the first race of the season and considered the crown jewel of NASCAR; Ford wanted to win it badly. The expression, "Win on Sunday, Sell on Monday" was the mantra in the corporate boardrooms.

Bill France was doing everything he could to fill the grandstands and, at the same time, pacify the major car manufacturers so they would race at his speedways and tracks. The rules were changing constantly, then as now. Of course, fudging and rule bending occurred; not all car manufacturers were totally satisfied, and rightly so. Moreover, when the manufacturers weren't happy, they boycotted the races.

By 1964, Chrysler had 30 years of experience; 5 were at Daytona and they were making the most of it. At this time, the Chrysler Hemi-equipped cars were the ones to beat, and Ford really didn't have a competitive powerplant in the lineup. This latest and fastest version of the Chrysler Hemi was introduced in Plymouth and Dodge stock cars just before the 1964 Daytona 500. Chrysler fitted its 426-ci big-block with well-designed, well-engineered hemispherical heads. Because this engine was not yet available in production cars, (technically, at least) it shouldn't have met any NASCAR rule. However, according to Bill France, because the engine (or its parts, that is, heads) were available over the parts counter, the engine could run in the event. The people at Ford cried foul, to no avail. This new Chrysler engine was unveiled at the last minute. It produced far more horsepower than Ford's 427-ci engine with the conventional wedge heads.

It wasn't long before the crew in the Ford and Mercury camp realized that during practice sessions, the Plymouth and Dodge cars were running at least 5 mph faster than their best times. Once again, Ford met with Bill France, voicing a valid complaint that, unfortunately, fell on deaf ears. The entire race became a Mopar show with the Hemi 426–powered cars finishing 1, 2, 3, and 4. Needless to say, Ford felt robbed by a rule change.

Ford, after all, had been focusing on European racing for the past few years. Now it was back home and wanted to offer up some winning Fords on the NASCAR circuits. At first, Ford offered a high-rev kit for the 427-ci engines, hoping to be competitive with the Chrysler Hemi. That didn't prove successful, so Ford went off the track and used political pressure to even the playing field.

At about that time in 1965, Chrysler produced the street Hemi, which was banned because of the incredible speeds it produced. This stock Hemi 426 was referred to as the elephant engine because it turned out 600-hp on the Dyno in the stock configuration, and even more in the race-ready form. Finally, Bill France stepped in and said, "Enough." Mopar responded by boycotting half the 1965 season; Ford boycotted part of the season the following year. Chrysler was allowed back in 1966 and won most of the races.

NASCAR leadership and France, in particular, were philosophically opposed to the 427 Cammer. His goal was to rid the sport of special racing engines because they created "non-stock cars." Ford was not quick to take no for an answer from NASCAR, and many at Ford thought that their company was being treated unfairly. The Cammer engine was the only big-block in Ford's arsenal capable of competing with the Hemi. It had a complex top end and timing chain setup, but it was essentially a reworked FE 427 2-valve hemi head.

Ford did not give up easily and tried to have the engine approved for the 1966 season. After several years of concerted efforts, NASCAR approved it for competition, but assessed such a severe carburetion restriction and huge weight penalty that the engine was rendered uncompetitive. Ford gave up trying to race the Cammer in NASCAR, but the engine dominated many experimental and factory classes in NHRA drag racing.

By 1967, the handwriting was on the wall. If Ford

Fran Hernandez, developer and manager of the Mercury Comet racing program, became the production manager for the Boss 429 program. (Photo Courtesy Fran Hernandez Collection)

was going to be competitive and win on the tracks, especially Daytona, it needed a new engine design. Moreover, all of the players needed to agree on the rules. After several heated meetings, almost everyone agreed on the rules, the first of which was no engine size larger than 7 liters (430 ci).

Over the years, a large and loyal fan base developed a tremendous interest because of its unique race history and rarity. The Boss 429 was only produced during a two-year period and in limited numbers. They are considered highly collectible today and the value of the remaining cars has consistently gone up yearly. As a street machine, they were difficult to tune and expensive to maintain. It was not unheard of for a new owner to pull out the exotic Boss engine and replace it with a 427 or 428 that was more suited to run on the street. Today, collectors are trying to match the available Boss 429 engines with the cars in which they were originally fitted at the Kar-Kraft facility some 46 years ago.

This strong and growing interest from collectors has produced impressive auction prices. Several of the cars have sold at the Barrett-Jackson auction in the last few years, bringing as much as $575,000. Some have been restored to an extremely high level and many have been modified for racing. I will explain how to identify and verify that a Boss 429 is the real thing and not a copy.

The Boss 429 engine has been used for a number of high-performance applications from NASCAR to drag racing to road tracks. It was a marketing stroke of genius to put this huge newly designed engine into an already exciting muscle car. The public took notice and bought the Boss 429 cars. They also bought other Mustang models; 1969 and 1970 were banner sales years.

FRAN HERNANDEZ AND FORD TOTAL PERFORMANCE

Francisco "Fran" A. Hernandez was one of the unsung heroes of this era. Born in 1922, Fran served a stint in the Navy during the World War II. When the war was over, he returned to Southern California, where he turned his passion for hot rodding into a full-time career. He became a machine shop owner with Fred Offenhauser and a foreman for Edelbrock Equipment. Fran was one of the first to use nitromethane in 4-cylinder engines. He was racing and winning with a 1932 Ford Coupe. He also worked for Bill Stroppe, who was building race cars, and Peter DePaolo, an Indy 500 racer. Fran became involved with Ford Motor Company racing through this connection.

He later got a job with the Electric Auto-Lite Company (later known as Autolite), which Ford eventually purchased. It didn't take his new company long to recognize his real talent. In 1960, Fran became known as the Man from Mercury after creating a performance-racing program for Ford's Lincoln-Mercury division. At this time, Mercury was involved in NASCAR racing, but it wasn't doing well, and in 1965, it stopped backing full-size stock cars.

"The full-size Mercury is too big for success in that kind of racing. It's like driving a school bus," said Fran. "There's no sense in going racing if you can't win. You're just wasting money. To race the Comet, under present rules, we'd have to have a 405-ci engine, and we don't build one." Therefore, it went drag racing with the Comet. Ford later sponsored the Comet Cyclone Funny Cars driven by Ed Schartman and Ron Leslie.

In 1964, as head of the Performance and Evaluation Department, Hernandez promoted the Mercury Comet by creating a 100,000-mile endurance run. The follow-up was the development of the Comet Cyclone GT for drag racing. Looking for more promotional opportunities, Hernandez built five 1964 Comets for the East African Safari race, which covered 3,000 miles of rough roads. This was a first for any American automaker and the publicity was tremendous. Fewer than 15 percent of the vehicles entered finished the race. "One of the Comets finished in 21st place," said Hernandez. "Not bad for a first try." He followed this event with another endurance run from Cape Horn at the southern tip of South America to Fairbanks, Alaska.

When it came to promoting the Mercury competition cars, Fran Hernandez was a visionary. He was a smart engineer and a top car builder, but he also knew where the future was when it came to marketing and car sales.

"In just a short time, half the population of the country will be 25 and under. The drag strip is the best place to show them the potential of our vehicle and our engine," he said, "We're not thinking so much of sales today and tomorrow, as sales in the future." This was 1966.

"He was a great engineer," said mechanic Bud Moore, whose South Carolina team, Bud Moore Engineering, built NASCAR racecars. "He understood what the drivers wanted. He was a real big help to us because he knew what needed to be done. It was a great honor to have him working with us."

CHAPTER 1

THE BOSS PROJECT AND VEHICLE IDENTIFICATION

The iconic Boss 429 Mustang has survived the test of time and is more popular and more valuable today than ever. With the value constantly climbing, these cars have become a good investment for collectors.

By the end of 1967, having performed very well on the racetracks of Europe, and winning the World Manufacturers' Championship, Ford, under Henry Ford II's direction, had achieved its goal of beating Ferrari. Therefore, Ford disbanded the European racing effort and shifted its attention to the home front, which meant NASCAR. The times were changing, as were the NASCAR rules.

Ford felt that it was time for some personnel changes, so Leo Beebe was promoted out and Jacque Passino was put in charge of Ford Performance. This was a good move because Passino was well known in the Holman-Moody camp, which had worked closely with Ford in the not-too-distant past.

Next came the big move. Henry Ford II convinced Semon "Bunkie" Knudsen of Chevrolet to come over and become president of the Ford Motor Company. Long before coming to Ford, Knudsen had established himself as a staunch advocate of high-performance cars, stating that racing was an essential part of marketing cars. As general manager of the Pontiac division, Knudsen, along with John DeLorean, Jim Wangers, and others, was behind the development and creation of the 1964 Pontiac GTO, which is considered the first muscle car. This precipitated the muscle car movement in the early 1960s. Knudsen was also a dyed-in-the-wool NASCAR fan, and is credited pushing the Boss 429 NASCAR engine forward. Knudsen's favorite saying was, "Build what you race, and race what you build."

From the beginning, this was a very special, almost secret project. Ford developed this fantastic new engine and it was going into the newly designed Mustang. The idea was for Kar-Kraft in Brighton, Michigan, to modify at least 500 new Ford Mustangs to physically accept the new Boss 429 engines, which turned out to be somewhat of a challenge. All of the cars were exactly the same, except for color.

VEHICLE AND ENGINE IDENTIFICATION

The Boss 429 was a homologation special, and held a special spot in Ford's racing history. As such, properly identifying each car is of paramount importance and, in turn, registration and validation has become very important for protecting the investment. So where do you look for the numbers that tell you that this is a real Boss 429 Mustang? Start by opening the driver-side door and looking at the identification plate that is riveted to the door.

Each car that went to Kar-Kraft was assigned a NASCAR KK number that was placed above the VIN on

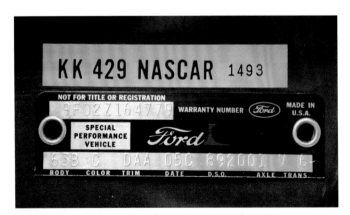

This door tag above the data plate identifies this car as a Boss 429, KK 1493. The Ford Motor Company data plate gives the following information for the serial number 9F02Z164779.

MUSTANG	RECOMMENDED TIRE SIZE and INFLATION PRESSURE (COLD)			
MODEL	ENGINE C.I.D. SIZE	STANDARD TIRE SIZE (LOAD RANGE B)	PRESSURE FRONT	REAR
NASCAR	429 H.O.	F60-15	24	24
FULL RATED (MAXIMUM) LOAD				
TOTAL LOAD - OCCUPANTS PLUS LUGGAGE				
MAXIMUM LOAD (LBS)	TOTAL OCCUPANTS	DISTRIBUTION FRONT	REAR	LUGGAGE
775	4	2	2	175 LBS
FOR SUSTAINED HIGH SPEEDS OR TRAILER TOWING – SEE OWNER'S MANUAL				

This NASCAR tire pressure sticker is on the driver-side door just above the data plate.

the driver-side door. By the end of the program, Ford and Kar-Kraft had produced 1,358 Boss 429 Mustangs over the two-year period. KK 1201 was the first Boss 429 Mustang; KK 2558 was the final car to roll out the door.

KK 1215 was the first car offered to the public. This means that KK 1201 through KK 1214 were engineering cars and engine development cars. Several cars went to important people within the organization. Car number KK 1205 was an example of an in-house car, and it went to Bunkie Knudsen. Another car, KK 1217, was a special concept car that eventually became a crash car. Used to test safety and collect crash test data, it was driven

9	1969
F	Built in Dearborn
02	Mustang 2-door SportsRoof
Z	429-4V Boss V-8 Engine
164779	Serial number of this Ford scheduled for production at Dearborn

63B	Mustang 2-door SportsRoof
C	Paint Code
DAA	Black Clarion Knit Vinyl Hi-Back Bucket Seats
05C	Scheduled for build date
892001	Transportation Services Ordering District under Domestic Special Order 2001
V	3.91 Trac-Lok Rear axle
6	4-speed close-ratio manual transmission

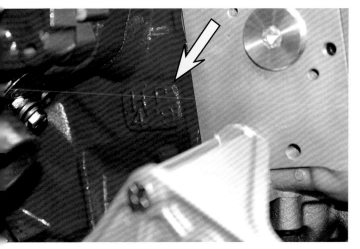

Check the front driver's side of the engine for "HP 429" in raised letters. This verifies that it is a genuine Boss 429 block. These engines have a special equipment package that includes four-bolt main bearings, a forged-steel crankshaft, and forged-steel connecting rods.

The serial number on this 429 block is located on the driver-side rear. The engine number and the serial number match, meaning that it's a numbers-matching car.

The casting number is stamped on the center housing of the differential.

into a barrier to see how it would hold up. The first 63 or 64 were high-priority cars that went to certain dealerships for sponsored racers. The invoice on KK 1279 shows that it went to Glen Organ Ford in Compton, California. At one time, Glen Organ was considered a high-performance and racing dealership; it sponsored Dan Gurney's 1964 or 1965 Galaxie in NASCAR racing.

According to Ford Motor Company, it lost several thousand dollars on each car built, but that was the cost of running the Boss 429 race program. The purpose was to get the 500 engines into the cars and out to the public to meet the NASCAR homologation requirement.

This Boss 429 has an HP block, and you can see the HP mark on the front of the block verifying its authenticity. Some of the mid- and late-1970s engines had what was called a mirror image 460 block. It was exactly the same block with no difference in the material. When Ford built an engine, several casting core boxes were used. From the very beginning, Ford used one casting core box for the front, two side boxes, a rear, and one that went down in the valley chamber.

Anytime there are rare cars, there is always a chance that someone will create a clone and try to pass it off as an original. That has happened at least once with the Boss 429 Mustang. When buying or selling, you need to do thorough research on the car because buying a Boss 429 is an enormous investment. You need to check the VIN, all identification numbers, and look it up in the

Lois Eminger was a long-time employee of Ford Motor Company and a car person. When Ford was preparing to destroy batches of invoices, Lois recognized the value of these vehicle records and asked if she could keep them. These invoices included some of the most popular cars of the 1960s and 1970s. Kevin Marti had been acquainted with Lois Eminger for 20 years. After she retired, she eventually sold the invoices and records to Kevin Marti. He continues the time-honored tradition of making those records available to rightful car owners. Although Lois passed away some time ago, her vision helped many people keep important original documentation.

Marti is the privileged licensee (contract number 5012) to Ford Motor Company's entire production database for the 1967–2007 model years. Marti can tell you everything about any Ford, Lincoln, or Mercury built in the United States or Canada during that period. What color was your car? Easy. What rear axle ratio? Sure. What day was the car sold? Yeah, even that, and a whole lot more. Unfortunately, data is not available for vehicles 1966 and earlier.

Ford used these original documents to bill the dealer. They contain the complete option list and, generally, the wholesale and retail costs of the base vehicle, all options, and shipping. These invoices also contain vehicle destination to the original dealer along with the trim code, date the invoice was prepared, and several other items.

According to Ford Motor Company, it lost $2,000–$4,000 on each car built. Ford personnel didn't care about that because the purpose was to get 500 engines to the public as quickly as possible. Thus, Ford met NASCAR's homologation requirements and the Blue Oval went back to what wins on Sunday, sells on Monday.

Looking at this, you can see that this car was scheduled for building on 1-31-69 (January 31, 1969), built on 1-31-1969, and released on February 19. The paperwork shows that it shipped on February 13, 1969. There's full documentation on all cars regarding when they were built and when they were shipped, etc.

Another interesting item, if you look at the original invoicing for each car, is that Ford couldn't release a car from the facility unless it was actually sold. So

The Marti Report tells just about everything that the car owner would want to know about his or her car.

all those cars were sold to Shelby American, and then they were released to the Kar-Kraft factory or facility, in Brighton, Michigan, where the work started. When the cars were finished, they were invoiced to the individual dealers. This was Ford's way of handling this particular program.

Please note that with the increasing value of these cars, many of these vehicles are now no longer just fun, vintage cars. Some are becoming part of automotive history. As such, the paperwork becomes an important part of that history. If you purchase any paperwork, please use adequate care to preserve it for posterity.

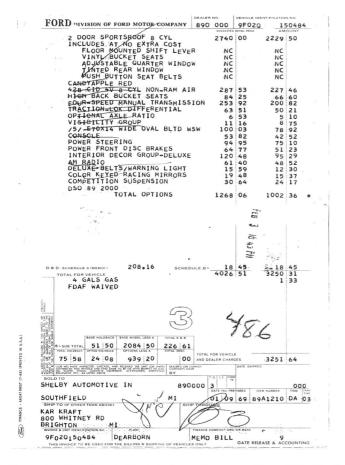
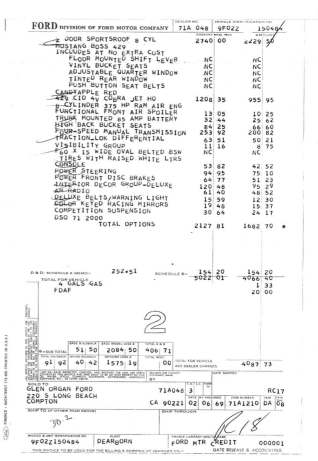

These two invoices tell a lot about the operation of Kar-Kraft. For example, there seem to be several different prices. Invoice no. 2 shows that the car (KK 1279) is going to a dealer, reflects the dealer prices, and the current price of items. Invoice no. 3 (KK 1279) obviously shows a wholesale price.

Most Boss 429s had a total list price of $5,022 and a sales amount of $4,066. In most cases, you could buy one of these cars for $3,600 or $3,700, depending on who you were and how badly you wanted the car.

Boss 429 registry. Full documentation is available on all Boss Mustangs, including when they were built, when they were shipped, to whom they went, and practically everything about the car, including the mileage.

There are several ways to verify a vehicle, especially a Ford. Marti Auto Works, a research firm, uses original Ford invoices, and can generate the paperwork and a complete report on the vehicle in question.

The Mercury Comets were well known on the drag strip but the full-size Mercury was meeting limited success on the NASCAR and USAC tracks. Ford was still promoting safety rather than performance.

At about the time that the baby boomers were getting their drivers' licenses, Ford realized that it was missing out on one piece of the pie: the performance market. Chrysler, Dodge, and General Motors were raking in this new group of customers because they cared less about safety than they did performance. It didn't take Ford long to change up its game plan and Lee Iacocca gets the credit for that.

For roughly the next 10 years, 1961 through 1971, Ford went all out with dedicated racecars and high-performance street cars, as well as with a wide range of racing parts and company sponsorship for top builders and racers, including Carroll Shelby. Ford even contracted with Shelby to produce the Mustang GT 350 and the GT 500. To help promote the cars, Hertz Car Rental had a number of Mustang GT 350s that anyone over the age of 25 could rent.

When Bunkie Knudsen went to Ford on February 6, 1968, he took Larry Shinoda, one of his top designers, with him. His mission was to improve the styling and sales of Ford's model-year lineup, but his role extended far beyond that. He played an integral role in the product planning for the Boss 429. However, Shinoda's first project at Ford was the Boss 302 Mustang and later the Boss 429, also known as the Boss-9. Shinoda had high regard for Knudsen and chose the name Boss in recognition, and also because Boss was popularly used to express cool and authoritative.

Another person who joined Bunkie Knudsen's racing efforts at Ford was master mechanic and engine builder Smokey Yunick. Smokey was not an employee but rather an independent designer, engineer, and shop owner contracted by Ford. Yunick was a self-taught engineer and one of the most creative and innovative racing minds of the day. He designed, engineered, and built competition cars for IndyCar, Trans-Am, and NASCAR racing. In fact, Smokey Yunick's cars won the Daytona 500 in 1961 with Marvin Panch and in 1962 with Fireball Roberts. When Knudsen enlisted the help of Smokey Yunick, he had an ace in the hole.

SELECTING THE MUSTANG

Ford developed and built the Boss 302 to homologate the car for Trans-Am road racing. Shinoda developed attention-grabbing graphics and body accents for the high-winding small-block. However, when it came to the Boss 429, Shinoda wanted a no-frills car and he styled it as an understated yet dedicated performance vehicle that was almost a sleeper.

Before the styling work began, Shinoda and the engineers met to discuss the Boss 429 project. Basically, they wanted to put this engine in the Galaxie because it had a large engine bay and would accept the huge engine easily. Moreover, it was for NASCAR, right? The Galaxie had been raced in NASCAR for years so it was the natural car for the engine. Ford could bolt the wide semi-hemi engine right into the car, sell them out of the dealerships, and go racing. But the burgeoning youth market was not interested in the staid full-size Galaxie, LTDs, and similar cars.

Mustang created the pony car market, and car buyers were buying compact and intermediate cars with potent V-8s. Shinoda and Hernandez knew that, so they discussed the marketing and the success of the Mercury Comet program. At this point, Shinoda took over and suggested they do something a little bit different this time. "If we put this new very different engine in the

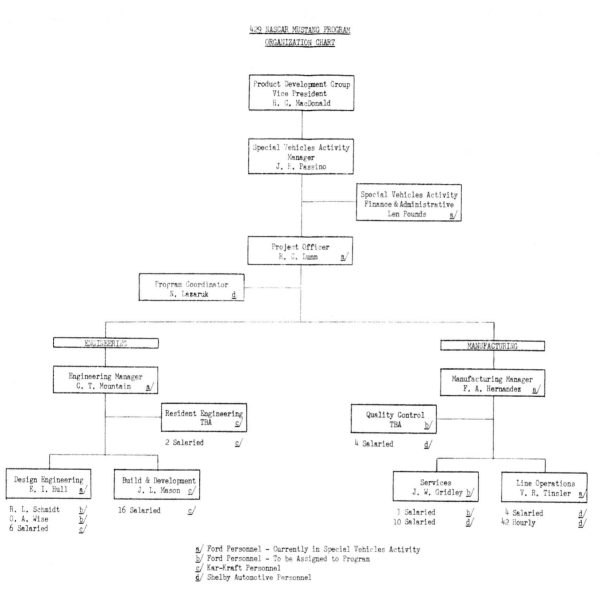

429 NASCAR MUSTANG PROGRAM
ORGANIZATION CHART

October 16, 1968

The Boss project required the best people Ford could assemble to make it a success. This confidential organizational chart for the 429 NASCAR Mustang Program, printed on October 16, 1968, identifies the key players involved in the program.

In 1970, when Ford no longer had a use for the building, a company called Rectrans, Inc., bought it to fabricate recreational vehicles. Rectrans, Inc., was started by Bunkie Knudsen with Larry Shinoda as vice president of design. Jacque Passino, manager of Ford Racing, was president of the company at one time. Larry followed Bunkie out the door to Rectrans after purchasing the old Kar-Kraft facility. In 1971, Bunkie went to White Motor Corporation, and as part of the deal, Rectrans was sold to White.

This is an aerial view of the Kar-Kraft building where Boss 429s were assembled. The complete assembly line was housed in this 65,000-square foot, 11-acre facility. (Photo Courtesy Fran Hernandez Collection)

Galaxie, no one is going to notice, except the stock car racing world, and our sales will likely stay the same.

"Let's go talk to Kar-Kraft and see if we can stuff the new engine in my newly designed Mustang. If so, we will have a sure-fire winner with the general car buying public."

Because the Boss 429 Mustang was more about an engine than an entire model, its design makeover was relatively simple. A large, almost square, functional scoop sat atop the hood, and the 1969 Mustang's phony side scoop and running horse emblems remained. The front spoiler resembled the Boss 302's, but there was no rear wing and no stripes along the fenders and doors, just outline letters proclaiming "BOSS" and "429."

KAR-KRAFT: FORD'S FACTORY SPEED SHOP

Kar-Kraft in Brighton, Michigan, was the company Ford hired to do all of its concept cars, special project vehicles, and race cars. The facility, located at 800 Whitney Avenue, Brighton, Michigan, was a mobile home factory when it opened in 1950.

Located next to the railroad, it was the ideal place for Ford to build its specialty and racing vehicles. Kar-Kraft had a long and distinguished history of building a variety of specialty vehicles, including the Boss 302, GT-40s, Broncos, and many other cars. It was only natural to modify the facility in late 1968 to convert 428 CJ Mustangs into the Boss 429. One interesting experimental car built at Kar-Kraft was a mid-engine 429 Mustang, which was not a success. The car was "stolen" while on its way to the crusher and is believed to be somewhere in the Seattle area.

Many of the racing and sports car projects originated on a restaurant napkin from the mind of a racer who had a pretty good idea of what worked and what didn't. Carroll Shelby was a good example; he had lots of hands-on experience behind the wheel, and he knew how to get things done. With the exception of the Shelby Cobra and the Daytona Coupe, most, if not all, Ford racing projects either originated from or were built at the Kar-Kraft facility. Not open to the general public, and certainly not to the competition, the semi-secret facility was sometimes called the Ford Skunk Works, especially during the period when Shelby took over the GT-40 racing program. In addition, of course, Holman-Moody played a big part in this effort.

In late 1968, Kar-Kraft was gearing up for a new supervisor, none other than Fran Hernandez, known for his innovative ideas and for getting things done. The timing couldn't have been better because the next big project coming down the assembly line was the Boss 429. "He was a hands-on guy . . . the type of guy who was a doer, not a talker," said John Mulrine, a former Ford technician.

SELLING THE BOSS 429 MUSTANG

Even before the car was off the drawing board, the public relations and media departments were working up an extensive advertising program. For a good understanding of the marketing and sales strategy for the Boss 429 Mustang, it is necessary to go back to April 1964. The lowly Falcon was on its way out, sales were down, and a replacement was needed. Intermediate-sized cars, such as the Pontiac GTO, had slotted a big 389 V-8 into the small car, giving other Detroit manufacturers a blueprint for the coming muscle car era. Ford didn't have anything with which to compete, but it had a ton of leftover Falcon parts.

Lee Iacocca, Ford's General Manager, was smart and wanted Ford to bring back a small sports car along the lines of the 1955–1957 Thunderbird. The powers that be didn't like the idea at all, but they would consider a 2+2, that is, two full-size bucket seats in the front and two smaller seats in the back. Something bigger than just a two-seat sports car would appeal to a larger buying market, and that would be the secret to success.

Calling it the pony car, Iacocca introduced several variations of the new concept at all of the major new

Shelby Mustangs are still very popular as SCCA club racers.

car shows. With media hype at its highest, he unveiled a new 1965 model. It was built on the compact Falcon, which lowered production costs and used up that surplus Falcon inventory. (The first cars were actually marketed as 1964½ models, as the lead-in to the 1965 models.)

This new pony car, the Mustang, was aimed squarely at the young market. A 170-ci 6-cylinder powered the entry-level model, and was aimed at the young female market, according to Iacocca. For those wanting more power, (read young male market), the options included two different V-8 engines.

At this point, Iacocca could do no wrong. The new Mustang sold more than 22,000 cars its first day out, with more than one million in sales in its first two years. The fresh new design and the price point, combined with the available options, made the car a lasting success and generated a loyal following, especially with the performance crowd.

Next, Ford introduced the new K-code 271-bhp, 289-ci V-8 and the performance crowd was hooked. Not done yet, Ford contracted Carroll Shelby to design modifications to the Mustang, so it would qualify as a sports car under SCCA rules. Shelby made the modifications by removing the rear seat, refining the suspension along with several other changes, making it fully race ready. Shelby and Ford called the new Mustang the Shelby GT-350, a Mustang fastback modified to meet the required specifications and specially tuned by Shelby and his crew. The stock 289-ci V-8 produced 306 bhp, but after going through Shelby's shop, was rated around 360 bhp.

The next big thing from 1966 through 1968 was the addition of a Paxton supercharger on the Hertz Rent-A-Car, known as the Shelby GT-350H, which was popularly called the Hertz Rent-A-Racer. The Paxton supercharger increased horsepower by as much as 40 percent. As anyone can imagine, every young man of at least age 25 was renting his dream car for the weekend. Not surprisingly, many came back the worse for wear after having spent the weekend at the local drag strip or racetrack.

Shelby enjoyed a milestone year in 1967. It was the year that the Shelby Mustangs were actually built by Shelby-American. After that, Ford built the cars with very little Shelby-American involvement.

For 1968, the Mustang became a real muscle car. The 428 Cobra Jet was an optional engine intended for the race group. Unlike the regular 428, it featured the larger valve heads and the competition intake manifold from the 427-ci engine. It also included an oil-pan windage tray to keep oil on the bearings at all times. This car also featured a hood scoop that actually funneled the air into the carburetor.

The Mach 1 body style debuted in 1969 and was standard with a 351-ci V-8 right off the showroom floor. For just a few dollars more, you could upgrade to the 428 Cobra Jet. Also available, on special order, was the Super Cobra Jet, which came with the Drag Pak option. This option included the limited-slip 3.91:1 or 4.30:1 rear axles, specially balanced nodular iron crankshaft, high-performance connecting rods, added engine oil cooler, and "Shaker" hood scoop. Air conditioning was not available with the Drag Pak option.

Ford had an impressive Mustang advertising and marketing record, and the over-the-top Boss 429 was practically a natural. Engines were sent to Holman-Moody to be modified for NASCAR, and the first few cars off the assembly line were sold to dealers involved in the racing program. The print and media coverage was non-stop. Ads were in every major magazine, and cars were made available to all major car and hot rod-type publications for testing and run comparisons. Journalists were flown to every major event to provide coverage, and other events, such as press days ensured the maximum amount of coverage possible.

This Mustang appealed to the public because it promoted a sporty lifestyle. Sales for the whole line of Mustangs were very good for 1969 and 1970. However, the reality was that Ford was selling the sizzle, not the steak.

In 1970, Ford added white as an interior color, but as you can see, this Boss 429 is black. This particular car also has the Deluxe interior package, which features woodgrain dash and upgraded gauge cluster and clock. In addition, the Boss 429 received a locking steering column in its final year.

The first year of the Comfort-Weave knitted vinyl seats was 1969. The cars came with deluxe seatbelts.

LIMITED OPTIONS LIST

As a no-frills limited-production performance vehicle, no options were available other than standard and mandatory equipment. Every Boss 429 Mustang that came off the assembly line at Kar-Kraft was the same, with the same equipment, with the sole exception of body color.

For 1969, here's what was on the build sheet:

- Boss 429-ci V-8 Engine
- High-Capacity Engine Oil Cooler
- 85-Amp Alternator
- 85-Amp Battery Mounted in Trunk
- Power Steering with Oil Cooler
- AM Radio (only)
- 4-Speed Close-ratio Gearbox*
- Power Front Disc Brakes/Rear Drum Brakes
- Trac-Lok Rear Axle with 3.91:1 Ratio**
- Special High-Performance Suspension***
- Front Spoiler****
- F60x15 Super Wide Oval Fiberglass Belted Tires
- Magnum 500 15 x 7-inch Chrome-Plated Wheels
- Tachometer
- Interior Décor Group
- Console
- High-Back Bucket Seats with "Comfort-Weave" Vinyl*****
- Dual Racing Mirrors
- Visibility Group
- Deluxe Seat Belts
- Manual Choke and Hood Scoop Control

*The Boss 429 Driveline features a high-performance clutch and pressure plate driving through the Ford full-synchro 4-speed transmission. Gear ratios are first: 2.32:1, second: 1.69:1, third: 1.29:1, fourth: direct, reverse: 2.32:1

**As mentioned above, the rear axle for the Boss 429 incorporates the "Trac-Lok" feature as standard equipment. The standard ratio is 3.91:1.

***The Boss 429 suspension features ultra-heavy-duty Gabriel front and rear shock absorbers, with the rear shocks in the staggered configuration to reduce wheel hop on full-throttle starts. In addition, the Boss 429 features both front and rear stabilizer bars to dampen out pitch and roll on cornering.

****The cars actually came with a front spoiler that was in the trunk; it was mounted after the car arrived at the dealership. This was because the spoiler was lower than the undercarriage of the car and would actually be ripped off during loading onto the convoy truck.

*****The all-black interior is fully carpeted and features the above-mentioned high-backed bucket seats covered in Ford's Comfort-weave knitted vinyl. The interior is quieted by the special Mustang Mach 1 sound insulation package.

Ford was producing these cars while Kar-Kraft was modifying them and installing the new Boss engines as fast as it could. Each car was slightly different, because of the way they were built. Build quality and assembly details vary from car to car.

By the end of the program, Ford had produced 1,358 cars over the two-year period. Larry Shinoda was right. The public took notice and Boss 429 Mustangs sold as fast as they became available, becoming the most illustrious and sought-after big-block Mustang ever built.

One night in November 1970, without notice, the curtain came down on the last act. Ford very quietly locked the doors to the Kar-Kraft facility and the run was over on the Friday after Thanksgiving 1970. Later, it came out that Henry Ford II felt that the expense was too much and did not translate into new vehicle sales. It seems that was only part of the story. In addition to the cost overrun, some accounting discrepancies contributed to the demise of the project. Shortly after that, Bunkie Knudsen, Larry Shinoda, and Jacque Passino all left Ford, and the short run of the iconic Boss 429 became another chapter in Ford history.

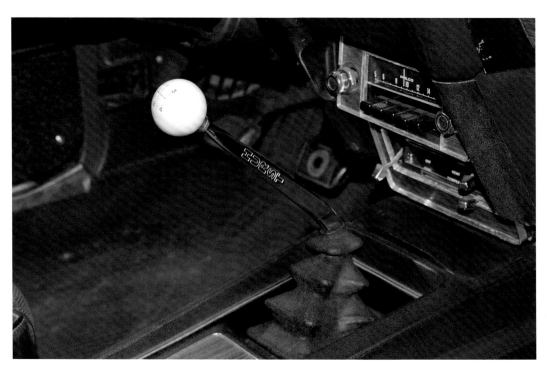

The Hurst shifter was standard on the 1970 models.

HOMOLOGATING THE BOSS 429 FOR NASCAR RACING

When Ford wanted to use the new Boss 429 engine in NASCAR competition, it had to follow the requirement to produce at least 500 cars with the new engines available to the public. This process is homologation. So what does that really mean? According to the dictionary, homologation, from the Greek *homologeo*, means "to agree." This is the granting of approval by an official authority, which may be a court of law, a government department, or an academic or professional body. Any of these authorities would typically work from a set of strict rules or standards to determine whether such approval should be given. The word may be considered loosely synonymous with accreditation, and in fact, in French and Spanish it may be used with regard to academic degrees. Certification is another possible synonym, while to homologate is the infinitive verb form.

In today's marketplace, for example, a public agency often ensures that products meet certain standards or are homologated for standards such as safety and environmental impact. A judicial authority may sometimes homologate a court action before it can proceed, and the term has a precise legal meaning in the judicial codes of some countries.

In motorsports, a vehicle must be homologated by the automobile sanctioning body to race in a given league, such as NASCAR or other sports car racing series.

When a racing class requires that the vehicles raced be production vehicles only slightly adapted for racing, manufacturers typically produce a limited run of such vehicles for public sale so that they can legitimately race them in the class. These vehicles are commonly called homologation specials.

Kar-Kraft as it looks today. One of the most recent businesses to use the facility is a company that makes fences and gates. (Photo Courtesy Fran Hernandez Collection)

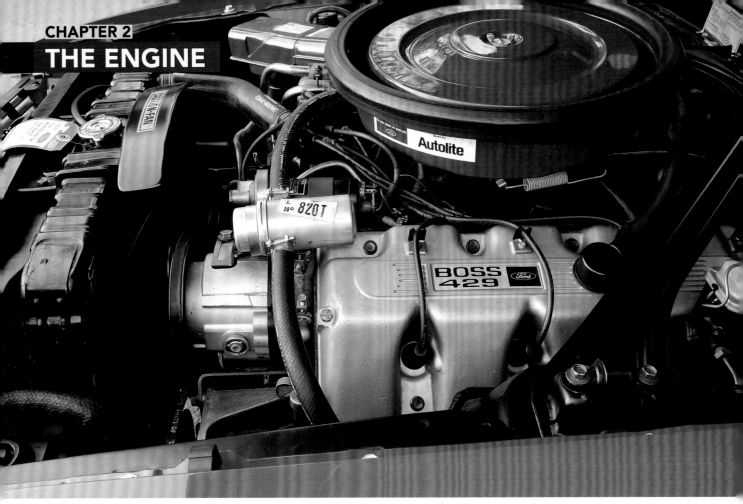

When the hood is opened, that big engine draws attention, and people quickly notice the size of the heads. The shock towers were cut and suspension geometry was modified to shoehorn the Boss 429 into the engine bay.

For Ford, the golden age of muscle cars lasted only from about 1964 to 1973, but this time was glorious and produced historic cars that are highly coveted today. This was a period when you could buy high-powered big-block 429/460 engines right off the showroom floor, and a lot of guys did. These cars could be driven on the street all week and, with very little modification, raced on the weekend. The Boss 429 was the pinnacle of the golden age of muscle cars. Race homologation specials and hand-built muscle cars coming out of a large facility such as Ford would never be seen again.

While the Boss 429 was similar to other 385 big-blocks, it had many distinct differences. It featured a different oiling system, thicker main bearing bulk-heads, and four-bolt main caps. In addition, push rod clearance was gained through block cutaways, and of course, the aluminum heads were unlike anything Ford had produced up to that point. The canted valves and massive 2.36-inch round intake ports flowed an enormous amount of air. The 2.28-inch-diameter intake and 1.90 exhaust valves were also huge. Other equipment worth noting were a forged steel crank, forged rods and pistons, and an aluminum intake manifold.

The Ford 429 engine was originally installed in Thunderbirds and LTDs in the mid-1960s. It didn't take long for the hot rod crowd to figure out that these engines had a lot of potential; soon they were showing up in more than just production cars. These engines developed a lot of low-end torque because they were designed to power a heavy car (the LTD) or four-wheel-drive truck. When a 429 engine was dropped into a much lighter car, such as the Fairlane, it produced impressive performance, even in stock configuration.

The 429 Thunder Jet was introduced in 1968; it was a basic passenger car wedge-engine design. It was designed with a hydraulic camshaft, two-bolt main bearing caps, and either a 2- or 4-barrel carburetor. The 429 Cobra Jet (CJ) was basically the same engine, but with a hotter hydraulic camshaft, a bigger carburetor, and larger heads with bigger valves. It should be noted that the Cobra Jet was fitted with two-bolt main bearings in 1970, but four-bolt main bearings in 1971.

The 429 Super Cobra Jet (SCJ) could be modified easily for serious competition right off the showroom floor. The 429 SCJ had four-bolt main caps on number 2, 3, and 4 journals, a mechanical camshaft with adjustable non-positive stopped rocker arm studs, stamped rocker arms, and pushrod guide plates. The pistons were forged aluminum, and connecting rod bolt seats were spot faced, and as with the CJ, production ended in 1971. As far as Ford big-block street performance cars were concerned, this ended the golden era.

The Boss 429 falls into this group (arguably), but with its unique equipment package, it truly stands on its own as a race engine designed to meet homologation standards. Of course, as part of meeting those requirements, it was heavily detuned for sale to the general public. However, even though the Boss 429 engine was a superior race engine, it demonstrated that the factory setup was not ideal for stoplight-to-stoplight street duels. These engines were typically advertised at 375 hp, but it was not unheard of to put one on the dyno and have it show in the neighborhood of 480 to 520 hp. The race engines that Holman-Moody put out were pumped up to the range of 620 to 640 hp.

Street performance for the Boss 429 suffered because of smog equipment. In addition, it was fitted with a restrictive low-rise intake manifold, a restrictive 735-cfm Holley carburetor, restrictive factory exhaust manifolds, and a mild camshaft. Moreover, the 1970 street models had a rev limiter. Ford's new smog equipment was the Thermactor clean air system, and a street version was used on the Boss

The iconic Boss 429 engine was used for stock car drag, boat, and other disciplines of racing. It didn't take the hot rod crowd long before they were building speed equipment for this new engine.

429. This exhaust emissions control system used an air pump that delivered fresh air to the exhaust port. There, it combined with the hot unburned carbon monoxide and hydrocarbons to complete the reduction of harmful gases. Major components of the Thermactor system are a belt-driven air pump, check valves, rubber hoses, as well as an air distribution manifold for each bank of cylinders and air injection tubes. "It's no wonder they didn't light up the asphalt as expected," said Denny Aldridge, "A good-running 428 Cobra Jet would run circles around the Boss 429 in street trim."

Even designer Larry Shinoda was disappointed with the final results. He had hoped for a street model that would do 10 seconds in the quarter-mile, which, of course, didn't happen. However, the engine had potential; it just needed some massaging to reach it. According to Denny Aldridge, "By doing the things that most racers did back then, change out the distributor, the carburetor, use the high-rise manifold, use decent headers, you can easily get 500 hp out of this engine."

On the competition side, Ford thought it had a winning combination with the highly successful and very reliable FE 427-ci engine. It dominated at European racetracks and was doing well in other arenas, such as NHRA and AHRA drag racing. On the NASCAR circuit, the only real fly in the ointment was Chrysler's Hemi, which looked unbeatable. Even with the new rev kit, the tried-and-true 427-powered Fords and Mercurys were no match for the Plymouth/Chrysler–prepared stock cars.

As mentioned, Bill France was no help with his vague rules. According to Smokey Yunick, France could disqualify years of work by simply saying it didn't meet the spirit of the sport. Ford was furious that its overhead cam idea was rejected. The Blue Oval was determined to come up with an engine that would meet the NASCAR rules and dominate on American race-tracks. That engine turned out to be the Boss 429. It was designed, produced, and introduced to the public in a last-minute last-ditch effort to remain competitive. Cost was not a consideration for this project. Winning at any cost and satisfying Ford's ego was the driving force behind it. Selling cars to the general public was import-ant, but in this case, it was almost secondary to winning.

Born out of desperation, the Race Experimental department of Ford's Engine and Foundry Division developed the Boss 429 engine. The engine research and development crew considered it nearly exotic. Its cast-iron cylinder block had four-bolt main bearings, but its heads were unusual; it was the most peculiar and complicated engine to ever come off the Ford assembly line. It also came with its share of problems.

Although its official name is the Boss 429, in the beginning it was called the Porcupine, the semi-hemi, the Blue Racer (after the Blue Oval), the blue crescent (the shape of the cylinder heads), and the Ford Shotgun (the size of the valves' holes). Engine bore and stroke was 4.36 x 3.59 inches. Normal oil pressure was 50 psi at 2,000 rpm. Holman-Moody developed an oil restric-tor kit to solve the oil system problems.

The original Boss 429 engine had an HP block. If you're looking to buy a Boss 429, you need to verify that this des-ignation was cast into the block. In the mid- and late 1970s, Ford produced the mirror-image 460 block. It was exactly the same block; there was no difference in the material.

When Ford built an engine, several casting core boxes were used. From the very beginning, Ford used one casting core box for the front, two side boxes, a rear, and one that went down in the valley chamber. Ford was able to change any or all of these casting core boxes to make a variety of changes such as changing the date codes on the block. There are multiple styles of Boss 429 blocks and they are all genuine. For example, the NASCAR block has all of the O-rings in the block rather than in the cylinder heads.

ENGINE VARIATIONS

Every component that Ford cast bore a code. To be perfectly clear, the casting number was not the part number. Ford's system was this: the date code followed

This Boss 429 block with 4-bolt mains is dated March 31, 1969. The HP identifier on the block is found at the front, back, and two spots underneath the block, up in the crank area. This is an early block and the casting core boxes had not been broken up yet. Ford also cast other blocks such as the mirror-image blocks.

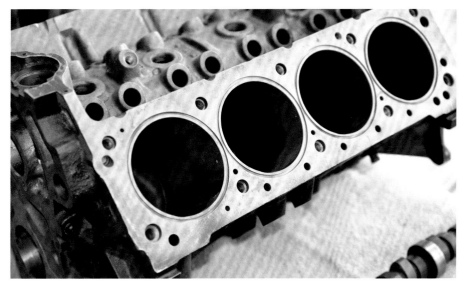

It is easy to identify this NASCAR block because it has the O-ring cut into the block, not into the head. The date code on the block is 9J27, which is September 27, 1969. It has a 460 image on the front of the casting, and inside it has the mirror image 460. This means that Ford used a different casting core box when casting this engine block.

the casting number, which was in turn followed by the code for who actually did the castings (that is, the company to which the project was outsourced). This system was the same for the intake manifold, the timing cover, etc. Even the cast-aluminum intake manifold has numbers. All of the information is on every part. That's why you can simply look at a part and see the whole history; you'll know exactly what it is as well as its year, month, and day of casting.

The Boss 429 engine had several different production runs, and the legendary Z-code engine has three variants. The 820S- and 820T-code engines were released in 1969; the 820 A-code followed in 1970. Each engine has an aluminum tag on top identifying it. Ford built 279 units in the initial 820S run. This NASCAR version featured hydraulic camshaft, magnesium valvecovers, as well as heavy-duty crank, rods (with 1/2-inch rod bolts), and pistons.

Released in mid-1969, engines numbered 820T still carried a hydraulic camshaft, but Ford reduced the weight of the rotating assembly, so it was a faster-revving engine that was better suited for street service. The very early versions used both the hydraulic and solid camshafts and magnesium valvecovers; eventually, aluminum valvecovers were installed. This engine used 3/8-inch rod bolts, as did both the 1969 and 1970 Boss 429s. In 1970, Ford introduced the

Although it's rusty, this is a brand-new in the box raw Boss 429 crankshaft from the Smokey Yunick collection that was purchased some years ago. This is the first time this box has been opened since its arrival at the Aldridge facility.

This crankshaft has a lot of surface rust. I got down on my hands and knees to do some close-up photography and found the serial number. After wiping it off with a little bit of water, a very rare XE serial number became visible. This is a special Holman-Moody crankshaft built specifically for racing. This divot is the result of a Rockwell test, which is a test for hardness. A designated testing lab uses a diamond mounted on a weight that is then dropped from a predetermined distance. The depth of this little divot indicates the hardness of the crankshaft steel, as per the Rockwell guidelines. This test was also performed on the 427 FE steel crank, the Boss 302 steel crank, and the Boss 429 steel crankshaft.

The NASCAR Boss 429 connecting rod (PN C9AX–B) used 1/2-inch bolts with 12-point aircraft-style nuts. This NOS connecting rod is unique because it has a yellow color code, which certifies that it has passed a Magnaflux test and is ready for installation in an engine. Note the part numbers.

Note the hole that goes through the length of the connecting rod. This supplies oil under pressure for the pin bushings.

820A version of the engine. It traded the hydraulic cam for a solid lifter cam and also featured lightened pistons, rods, and crankshaft. While some folks may prefer the more race-oriented mechanical-cam 820A, Boss 429s equipped with this engine are no more valuable than S- and T-engine cars.

The Boss 429 cylinder block used four-bolt main caps, stronger main bearing saddles, and an altered oiling system. According to Ford, "Advanced, thin-wall casting techniques had been used to provide reasonable weight and eliminate hotspots in the block. The five-bearing crankcase had the reinforcing bulkheads in line with each bearing. Double-bolted main bearing caps further reinforce the engine's exceptional bottom end."

The NASCAR blocks were no different from factory Boss 429 blocks, except for the O-rings cut in the top of the block deck. It's the same material, and the same casting technique as the stock factory unit. Holman-Moody sonic-tested these blocks to identify the thicker blocks, which went out to the race teams. Other than that, it's a regular Boss 429.

The rare thing about both blocks is that no serial number appears on either one. This is how you can tell that they have never been in a car because if they had been, they would have a serial number. This means that they were probably

Holman-Moody blocks, acquired by Aldridge during the big Holman-Moody sale when the company divested itself of all Boss 429 parts.

ROTATING ASSEMBLY

According to Ford, the crankshaft used in the Boss 429 engines is forged alloy steel. Before installation in the block, the crankshaft was electronically balanced, both statically and dynamically.

Three different crankshafts were installed in Boss 429 engines. The first, the Boss 429T, carries PN C9 AZ-6303CT. These crankshafts were used in street engines with standard Boss 429 connecting rods. The second crankshaft, the Boss 429S, was a NASCAR crankshaft, PN C9 AZ-6303-A. These were used in engines with NASCAR-type forged connecting rods; they had heavier counterweights for correct balancing. The third was a raw forged truck crankshaft. Made of 1041 material, it was originally forged for the big 385 series trucks, but was also used in the Can-Am series 494-ci race engines. These crankshafts show a dollar sign ($) and an "A." It is common knowledge that the 427 Ford, the Boss 429, and the Boss 302, had forged-steel crankshafts in their engines; that's what the dollar sign signifies.

The later solid lifter camshafts had the cut in the distributor gears, as does this; the early ones did not.

To verify that this is a new original Boss 429 camshaft, examine the back of the cam journal; the last lobe should have a FoMoCo insignia on it. You'll notice that it has green and orange color codes on it for the Boss 429. In addition, there are other letters called the backwards B and J, which also designated the Boss 429. This is a hydraulic lifter camshaft.

PARTS LIST FOR MECHANICAL TAPPET CAMSHAFT CONVERSION
429 CID BOSS BLUE CRESCENT ENGINE

Quantity	Part No.	Part Name
1	C3TE-9417 -A	Gasket - Fuel Pump
2	C9AE-9439 -A	Gasket - Intake Manifold
2	C8VE-9A425-A	Seal - Intake Manifold
2	C9AE-6584 -A	Gasket - Rocker Arm Cover
1	C8VE-6020 -A	Gasket - Front Cover
2	373030 -S	Clip - Fuel Line
16	DOAE-6500 -B	Tappet
1	C9AE-6250 -E	Camshaft
1	C8VE-6722 -B	Seal - Oil Pan (Front)
1	C3AE-6700 -A	Seal - Crankshaft
1	C8VE-6710 -A	Gasket - Oil Pan - R
1	C8VE-6711 -A	Gasket - Oil Pan - L

Camshaft conversion sheet.

These crankshafts were put on a production line and machined to a 3.85 stroke, the same as for a 460 Ford, to produce the 494-ci engine. This same stroke was used in the Boss 429 Funny Cars.

Because the crankshaft arrived raw, the rod throws could be turned down and then stroked to any desired size. An interesting note is that the Funny Car guys were running Chrysler aluminum connecting rods. Ford just turned the rod throws down to the same size as the Chrysler's and ran the Chrysler aluminum connecting rods (2.375 instead of 2.500), which was the standard Ford connecting rod size. Today, the Ford racers turn the rod size down to 2.200, which is that of the big-block Chevrolet.

Ford made stout connecting rods to handle its racing endeavors and to ensure that the rods could withstand continuous high-RPM punishment during NASCAR

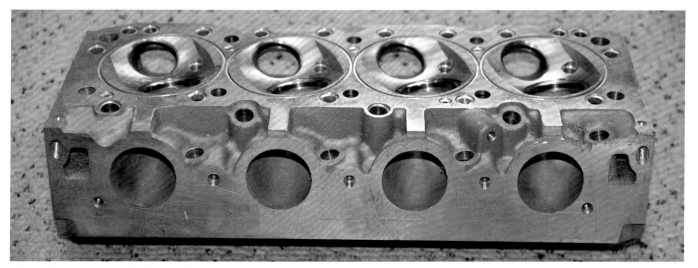

These aluminum cylinder heads feature the modified hemispherical-type combustion chamber, which Ford called "crescent." The intake port measured 2.23 x 2.36 inches, and the exhaust port measured 2.04 x 1.68 inches. The intake and exhaust valves were considered huge with the intake measuring 2.28 inches and the exhaust measuring 1.90 inches.

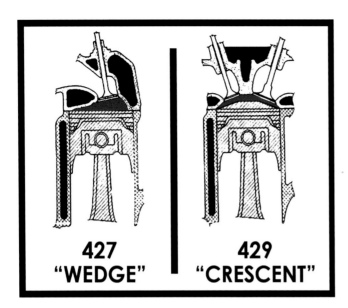

427
"WEDGE"

429
"CRESCENT"

The newly designed cylinder heads and pistons in the Boss 429 create a smaller and more efficient combustion chamber than the older 427 engines. The design unshrouds the valves for better heat transfer to aid in running higher compression ratios needed in competition engines. With both pistons at top dead center, it is easy to see that the red area, representing the combustion area, is smaller and more efficient in the Boss 429, thus producing more power than the older 427.

competition. The rod has a center rib that is not necessarily for strength. It has a pressurized oil passage that runs from the big end up through the beam to oil the wrist pin bushing; this is pin oiling. The bushing has a special groove that allows the oil to circulate and prevent it from burning up. Spray from this bushing was intended to cool the underside of the piston crowns. However, this spray cured another problem with the early engines, which was excessive wrist pin wear. This passage is not simply drilled through, as is a normal rod. A special forging is used that has a bulge along the side of the beam to house the drilling.

SOLID LIFTER CONVERSION

The first Boss 429s used hydraulic lifters, so oil was required to supply the tappets. Produced during the first part of 1969, the 820T engine carried a hydraulic cam and therefore hydraulic lifters. The fact is that they were actually 429 Cobra Jet camshafts that were on the shelf, so they were used first. They were used in the production-line cars.

In late 1969, after a number of complaints regarding lack of power, Ford decided that it could make more horsepower from these engines by using solid-lifter (or mechanical) cams. This new engine was designated as the 820S, for solid lifter cam. "S" versions used hydraulic

The Boss 429 combustion chamber is shown here with depth measurements. It is important to check the depth of the groove from the deck of the cylinder heads to the bottom of the groove. This is .063 inch at this point. I check the depth at every 90 degrees all the way around the head. This is on one cylinder head. When building an engine, both cylinder heads must be the same. This is called mapping.

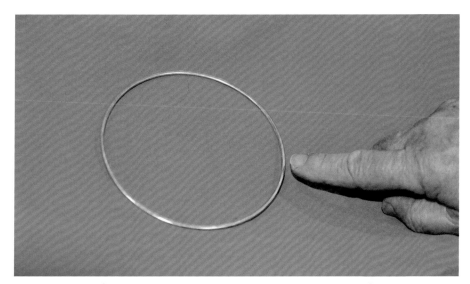

This is nitrogen-filled silver hermetically sealed–type "O" ring is the same type used in the 494–ci Can-Am engines. It ranges from .088 to .092 inch once it is crushed (between the head and the block.) These are not currently available.

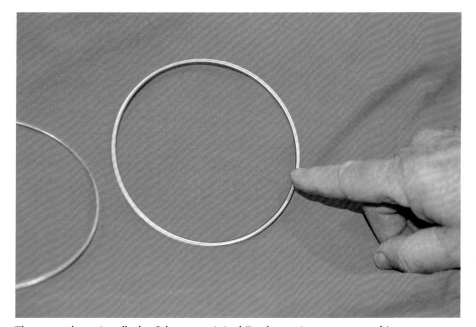

The second one is called a G-lap, an original Ford part. In most cases, this one runs from .085- to .093-inch thick. When the cylinder head is torqued to the block, they usually crush to around .070 to .075 inch. This is an extremely crucial measurement to remember when doing this installation.

cams; "T" engines later used solid lifter camshafts. These lifters simply transfer cam lobe action to the pushrod; they do not contain oil and are not self-adjusting. As a result, they require periodic adjusting. Valvetrains using solid lifters are prone to clicking or clattering as valves open and close.

At this point, Ford produced a three-ring binder titled, *Request for Publication Technical Service Bulletin* and sent it to all dealers. It supplied information on converting to the solid-lifter camshaft, what parts were required, and how to do it. Across the front of the first page in red ink was the handwritten underlined note: *Proprietary Information — Not for release to the general public at this time.* To facilitate the conversion from hydraulic to solid tappets, Ford provided screw-in plugs for the tapped holes in the block to seal off the oil supply to the lifters. Special plugs with O-rings were screwed into these holes to make the conversion.

Several different types of material were often used to make camshafts; the Boss 429 used chilled-iron castings. Commonly used in high-volume production, chilled-iron camshafts have a good wear resistance because the chilling process hardens the iron. Other elements are added to the iron before casting to make it more durable. Camshaft lobes are created using a precision machining process. The number of valves determines the number of lobes on the camshaft.

The next step in getting the head ready is to verify oil and water "O" rings depth. This larger "O" ring is about .069-inch thick, and is for the water while the smaller one is for the oil. These unique Viton-type rubber O-rings have a stainless-steel insert that is molded inside. These must be correctly installed so that the Boss 429-cylinder head doesn't leak.

VALVETRAIN

Here's what Ford engineers said about the Boss 429 engine: "The heads have extremely large, round, free-flowing ports that match up with a flowmeter-developed aluminum intake manifold and carefully shaped exhaust headers. The valves in the crescent curve of the heads are extremely large and placed transversely so that the intake valves are nearest the intake manifold and conversely the exhaust valves are to the outside or exhaust header side of the engine. This is a true crossflow position, which is a characteristic of the double overhead cam Ford engine and allows minimum breathing restriction.

By staggering the valves in this manner, there is substantial spacing between all exhaust valves, eliminating hotspot areas. A highly sophisticated chrome-moly cobalt steel alloy is used for the valve seat inserts in the aluminum head. These inserts are machined to extreme accuracy and, for assembly, are placed in dry ice to shrink the diameter. In this condition, they are pressed into the heated head recess forming a permanent bond. The inserts have exceptional durability and resistance to warpage."

The Boss 429 uses a chain and sprocket cam drive. The two camshafts used in the Boss 429 have a 296-degree .506-inch lift for the hydraulic lifters and a 300-degree .509-inch lift for the mechanical lifters. Both are 429 SCJ spec.

INTAKE AND EXHAUST

The Boss 429 heads have enormous ports designed to match up to a high-rise aluminum intake manifold. However, a high-rise manifold would not fit under the stock Mustang hood. The stock combustion chamber is 82 to 88 cc, while the full hemi conversion is 100 cc. Therefore, Ford went to the low-rise aluminum intake manifold. Unfortunately, the huge ports and low-rise intake manifold couldn't generate enough low-RPM air velocity, and torque suffered dramatically.

Fitting this huge engine into the Mustang's small engine bay required a lot of fabrication and compromises. One concession was the exhaust headers. They were designed to fit into a very tight space, rather than for performance.

The 1970 dual exhaust system was much better than the 1969 version. The 1969 Boss 429 had two resonators in front of the rear axle and a crossflow muffler behind the rear axle. The 1970 Boss 429 had two mufflers in front of the rear axle only and a freeflow through-system.

Exhaust header–type manifolds had large, round, inside dimensions and extended runner links that blended into a larger collection chamber to aid in the extraction of exhaust gases. Elimination of back-pressure is an important feature in net available power.

DRY-DECK CYLINDER HEADS

The street Boss 429 Mustangs were rated at 375 hp, with 450 ft-lbs of torque. Estimated actual output was somewhere in the 500-hp range. These engines were designed to run in the higher RPM range, and the 1970 street version was fitted with a 6,200-rpm rev limiter.

This was a race engine in a street car, and high-performance street cars benefit from torque rather than high-RPM horsepower. From that standpoint, the Boss 429 was not a good fit for a street car. This performance problem was an ongoing issue for cars sold to the general public. However, with correct tuning and a few necessary changes, the street model could deliver very impressive performance.

Ford elected to use the dry-deck construction method on these heads to maintain the high compression ratio and cylinder pressure because a race engine was designed to run at high RPM for long periods of time. Each cylinder, oil passage, and water passage had an individual

This 2.4-inch NASCAR intake valve has a yellow color code show that this was X-rayed, inspected, and approved for use in NASCAR. In addition, these have a number at the top that is a date code. This also tells you that these are the stainless-steel hollow-stem valves.

This new Holman and Moody piston has the intake pocket and the exhaust pocket cut into the top of the piston. These are tulip cuts. The valves have the same tulip shape and fit hand-in-glove with the piston tops. This particular piston is approximately 13.5:1 compression. Notice that off to the right is what is called a fire slot. For the race engines, this fire slot was opened up considerably. From a racing standpoint, the fire slot shown here is considered restrictive to the flame travel.

For each cylinder, it is possible to mill some off the area off or open up these crescents. (That's why they're nicknamed the "blue crescent.) Using a machining tool called a "bowl cutter," Holman-Moody removed these crescents and turned the cylinder head into a full-hemispherical chamber. As it is now, this is a semi-hemi head.

O-ring–style seal rather than a head gasket. In fact, rubber O-rings with steel inserts were used for the oil and water passages; a steel gasket sealed the combustion chambers. These are difficult to install correctly and they are costly. If they are not installed with the correct O-ring, they will leak.

The best way to explain this method is to show one of the heads and how it all fits together. Denny Aldridge has a set of NOS heads that came from "Ohio George" Montgomery, who successfully competed in NHRA drag racing with his twin-turbo Boss 429 drag car.

Two holes are in the side of this cylinder head. One is at the front

The intake ports were the biggest ever produced by Ford. They measured 2.36 x 2.36 inches, approximately the size of a tennis ball.

while the other is at the rear; the reason is somewhat of a mystery. According to Ohio George, Ford had the cylinder heads milled and then shipped the heads to him. However, Ford didn't have any 429 Boss blocks at the time, so it sent 429SCJ blocks instead. But they didn't have the correct oil drain-back holes in them. Ohio George had to use the heads to get his drag racing project running, so he drilled and tapped the holes in these heads for external oil drains that went from the heads to the oil pan. This allows these heads to be used on a 429/460 block, a 429 Cobra Jet, or a 429 SCJ block.

As mentioned, the Boss 429 used O-rings rather than a traditional head gasket for its dry-deck system. There are O-ring grooves for the water and the oil passages; the O-rings fit snugly in their grooves. After the O-rings for the cylinders are in place, the head is installed onto the block; the head bolts are then torqued to the proper spec. A feeler gauge is used to check for clearance around the edge of the cylinder head and at all four corners where it is mated to the block. There should be clearance; the correct reading is between .006 and .010 inch.

New cylinder O-rings are .090 to .092 inch thick. The groove in the NOS cylinder head is .062 to .063 inch deep. When preassembled and torqued onto the block, the cylinder O-ring holds the head off the block by approximately .010 inch, crushing the O-ring to approximately .070 to .080 inch.

NOS water and oil O-rings are gray Viton rubber with stainless steel inserts molded into the center. They measure .070 inch thick. If you look at the mapping, the water and oil grooves are .042 to .045 inch thick. You are checking the amount of preload or squish factor on the oil and water O-rings. It's important to

do the math after mapping or you will end up with a disaster and it will probably leak. If this procedure is not followed correctly, there's a very good chance that the oil/water/antifreeze will be squirting out between the head and the block when the engine is fired up.

Many Boss 429 blocks and cylinder heads have been damaged from extreme use. When repaired, these heads are often welded and machined, but not to the correct depth and size of the grooves. This welding and incorrect repair warps the heads and takes the heat-treatment out of the heads. A specific procedure is followed to correctly install the O-rings. When the O-rings are positioned in the head, silicone adhesive is applied to hold them in place. Using a silicone-caulking gun, go around the outside of the cylinder head, staying back from the edge approximately 1/4 inch. Next, a small bead of silicone goes around every O-ring before the cylinder head is installed. After the head is installed and torqued, the excess silicone that squeezes out is wiped away. This forms an automatic seal around the outside perimeter of the cylinder heads.

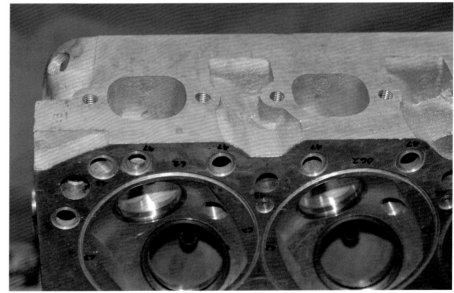

The exhaust port is D-shaped while the intake port is round. The exhaust ports measure 1.68 x 2.04.

39

The Engine
Chapter 2

Aftermarket rocker arms are considered bulletproof. These are the John Kaase rockers for his new competitive cylinder heads. The valvespring oil squirters were machined and installed by Aldridge Racing.

The first Boss 429 rocker arm assemblies were non-adjustable for the cast-iron experimental heads and the lash was set by valve-lash caps. The standard production rocker arms on 1969s and 1970s (shown) were adjustable to set lash.

Installing the head on the block is a two-person project. The full procedure for these engines is laid out in the Ford technical manual. Aldridge says, "I recommend cutting off two old 460 long-head bolts and put a screwdriver blade at the non-threaded end to help guide the heads onto the block. After heads are seated into the block, use a screwdriver to remove the alignment guides."

Ford states that the street and NASCAR Boss 429 cylinder heads use the same casting and are therefore identical regarding port sizes and combustion chamber configurations. However, the biggest difference is that the street heads have grooves in the face of the head for the combustion sealing rings. On NASCAR engines, these grooves are in the block.

Next is the 1.900 NASCAR exhaust valve. Most of these were sodium-filled hollow-stem valves. All parts were documented and inspected at Holman-Moody before use to ensure that they would hold up under racing conditions. Unfortunately, in some cases, they failed when used for racing.

The quench areas on the side of the combustion chamber were designed to provide better combustion.

This is a rare magnesium valvecover from the Smokey Yunick collection. It features the Ford script, and is one of only three sets ever made from the casting that Yunick created for Ford. I've only seen pictures of this on one car that was only for display. Magnesium was used because it is an incredibly lightweight material that greatly reduced the engine weight for NASCAR racing.

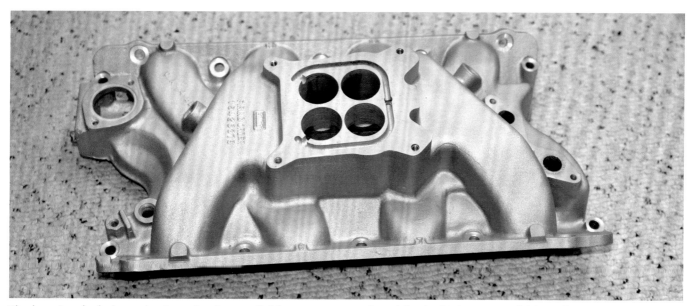

The low-rise dual-plane aluminum intake manifold was a compromise while the high-rise manifold would have provided better high-RPM performance.

This is an original (writing on the tag) 1969 Boss 429 carburetor. It's a single Holley 4-barrel carburetor, model number 9510, rated at 735 cfm. This double-pumper design features vacuum secondaries and a factory heat choke (model 4150, PN C 98F–9510–U). Note the stampings and the date codes on the tag.

These carburetors can be found at swap meets or sales. When examining one to verify that it is an original, open up the butterfly for the choke and look inside. The real Holleys have bell boosters in the front; the backside features down-leg boosters. The only carburetors configured this way are for the Boss 429 and the 428 Cobra Jet.

The original NASCAR Boss 429 carburetors ran on spider manifolds. They originally came with the choke, but the choke mechanism has been removed from this one. A list number of 4575 is the correct part number for the NASCAR unit, which means this is a fairly rare carburetor. These are mainly used on longer tracks.

It is easy to see why these heads, combined with the special pistons and oversized valves, made the Boss 429 such a fantastic engine. Ford had done its homework with the reinforced block, crankshaft, and connecting rods. Mounting these heads on this engine was absolutely brilliant. The spark plugs are Autolite AF–32; the gap is .035 inch.

When fitted together, the head is off the block by about .010 inch. Typically, the piston flats (top of piston) run approximately .010 to .020 inch below the deck of the block. Important items to consider are the RPM, the weight of the piston, and the amount of connecting rod stretch. They generally ran .020- to .030-inch piston-to-head clearance; that way, the piston wouldn't come up and touch the cylinder head.

These are aluminum heads with Stellite valve seats, a very hard material designed for wear resistance. These press-in seats absorbed a portion of the heat from the combustion chamber to dissipate the heat to the cylinder head, preventing the valve from destroying the aluminum cylinder head.

Like other 385 series engines, the Boss 429 is a traditional cam-in-block engine with a pushrod-actuated valvetrain. Because the pushrods passed through the cylinder heads in their common location, one short rocker arm (intake) and one long rocker (exhaust) reached the angle valves. Oil is supplied to the shaft-mounted rocker arms through passages in the block and heads, rather than through the pushrods as on the normal CJ429. In 1969 only, hydraulic lifters were

Holley offers this reproduction carburetor, mounted on a stock painted manifold. You can tell because it has no date code stamped on it. The reproductions are well done and the castings are very close to the original.

This Toploader transmission has big input and output shafts, with a short tail housing.

1969–1970 Ford Mustang Boss 429
In Detail No. 7

The serial number on the side of this Toploader is RUG AE, which indicates that it was built for the 1968 Mustang 428, the 1968–1969 Mustang and Cougar 428, and the 1969 Mustang 428 and the Boss 429. It also designates it as a close-ratio 31-spline unit.

used on the street machine. To maintain the precision of the valve timing, heavy-duty valvesprings were used along with individual shaft-mounted forged rocker arms.

In addition, the Boss 429 was fitted with a low-rise aluminum intake manifold so that the stock Mustang hood would clear the engine. However, the consensus was that a high-rise aluminum manifold produced a stronger fuel charge and was better suited for this engine.

The dual-plane, aluminum intake manifold (PN C9AE9425-D) features high-volume runners and a split plenum. The stock unit has different passages for the PCV valve, which ran off the back of the manifold. Because Ford didn't have a carb spacer to run the PCV valve, it ran the veins in the intake manifold up to the primary side so that the PCV valve would work correctly. In addition, the heat tubes come up from the exhaust manifolds to heat the carburetor. The high-volume runners in the intake manifold are carefully matched with the head ports to form as smooth and direct an entrance as possible.

TOPLOADER 4-SPEED TRANSMISSION

In 1963, the gigantic Boss 429 engine was mated to the extremely durable Ford Toploader transmission, replacing the older BorgWarner T-10. With

The serial number of the car and the matching transmission serial number are on top of the housing for the Boss 429. This transmission is for the original white Boss 429 KK 1668, part of the Aldridge collection.

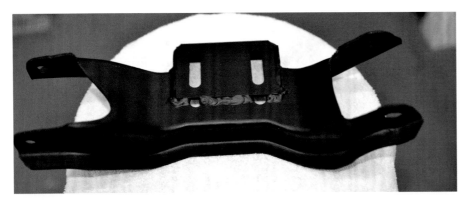

The Boss 429 transmission crossmember was modified from the original 428 cars. When these pieces arrived at Kar-Kraft, the new Boss 429 engines had been mounted farther forward in the car, so the mount was cut and a new plate was welded in the center.

The 1969 nodular Ford 9-inch differential was initially built for the 1964 Thunderbolts and was installed in 428 Cobra Jets. This very rare nodular 9-inch Ford differential was standard in all Boss 429s. They are now very much in demand, but are still available, mainly because Ford built so many of them. They were available in other Ford big-block cars that were being prepared for racing.

an easy 550 real-world hp on tap, a tough transmission was needed. For the Boss 429, this manually shifted 4-speed gearbox was up to the challenge and could handle that horsepower. It was fitted into many production street vehicles and was used extensively in racing, especially NASCAR.

This is the 3.03 Ford designed 4-speed, so-called because the centerline distance between countershaft and mainshaft is 3.03 inches. It earned the Toploader name because the access plate is located on the top of the main case and provides additional strength. Most manual transmissions have the access plate on the side of the transmission, rather than the top. The 24-inch Toploader 4-speed, like other transmissions, has fully synchronized gears. When the Ford engineers designed the Toploader, it was with two engines (applications) in

The squirrelly "N" is shown on the outside of the case. Eight different cases were produced from the 9-inch Ford rear end. The red oxide and the splash of yellow paint verify it as an original Ford nodular case, which was the strongest.

The letters and numbers on the inside of this nodular case read: N C4 AW-B. The N signifies nodular. C4 AW is the number of the casting core box and signifies 1964. The B stands for big bearing, which is the 3.16-inch carrier bearing. These cases were created for the 1964 Thunderbolt 427 high-rise engine because the previous cases were cast iron and prone to cracking.

The production date of this nodular case was September 15, 1969. The letters and numbers read: 9J15 (the numeral 9 has two dots under it so it can't be mistaken for the numeral 6). The 9 signifies 1969. The J signifies the ninth month because the letter "I" is not used. The number 15 stands for the day it was cast, the 15th day of the month.

mind: small-blocks such as the Ford Windsor engine, and big-blocks such as the FE engine and 385 series. To withstand the torque, some big-blocks, including the Boss 429, required a larger input shaft as well as the output tail shaft, which carries most of the torque.

The number 250 is stamped in the center of the transmission crossmember because it was used for the 250 6-cylinder engines even though it was originally meant to fit 390 and 428 engines.

The Boss 429's stout drivetrain featured the rugged and reliable Ford 9-inch differential. Because it was Ford's strongest and toughest differential for about 30 years, it was installed in a variety of pony cars, muscle cars, and trucks. The only case ever used with the Boss 429 was the nodular iron or "N" case, which was only available for high-performance Ford vehicles, having been specially designed for hard core racing, such as NASCAR and drag racing. It included larger carrier bearings and 31-spline axle shafts.

Some of the other 11 cases produced with the date code have a "SPEC." Ford stamping that designates them as "Special." These were used in the 1967 Shelby GT 500. Ford cast all of these in one casting core box. They use the same casting core boxes but just changed the date on the front; these were used through 1969.

These caps were also available in cast iron and really don't hold up under hard racing conditions, so it's extremely important to know what you are looking at. It's not uncommon for the cast-iron caps to come off under heavy or extreme performance.

In 1970, the case was changed to a D00W-B, which uses the small carrier bearing (also called a slim-line bearing; Timken PN 102 949 and PN 8102 910). The D00W-B case bears no mark, which indicates that it uses a small carrier bearing. If you look inside the case above the rear support bearing cases (C4AW-B), a "0" indicates that it uses the big bearing.

The Nodular iron Ford 9-inch was standard equipment for the Boss 429. "A" signifies Galaxie. An "O" indicated Torino or Fairlane; "Z" meant Mustang.

An "N" (nodular iron) on the carrier caps indicates that the differential uses the larger bearings. This is very important when picking out differentials, especially for racing or high-performance.

Even the Boss 429 Mustang had drum brakes in the rear. Disc brakes were up front because 80-percent of the stopping power was there with only 20 percent in the rear. Shown here is a heavy-duty drum with the fins.

CHAPTER 3

CHASSIS AND SUSPENSION

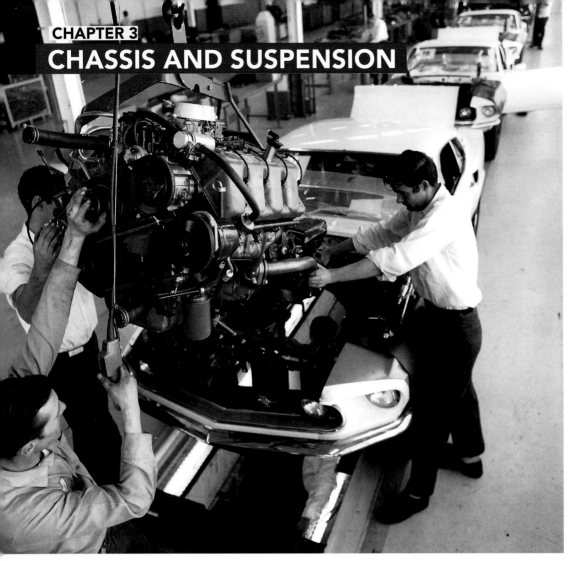

It was almost an art: installing the engine, connecting all the wires and hoses, and getting it running. The two members of the crew working below are fitting the new suspension and making sure that it has enough clearance for everything to operate correctly. (Photo Courtesy Ford Images)

The 1969–1970 Ford Mustang fastback was a small car, and the Boss 429 engine was too large for the stock engine bay. It was going to be an engineering challenge to shoehorn that huge engine into this sporty, smaller car.

Fran Hernandez sat down with his team of engineers and mechanics and worked out a design that allowed them to modify these cars in the least amount of time without visibly altering the exterior appearance. These were purpose-built cars, and as such, required substantial modification before they would be finished.

To make the transformation a little easier, all Boss

429s were ordered as Q-code cars, which meant that they were equipped with a non-ram-air 428 Cobra Jet with an engine oil cooler. They were fitted with a Toploader 4-speed close-ratio 2.32 transmission and a rear end with a 3.91 Trac-Lok 31-spline axle. Using a plain-Jane Mustang fastback as the basis of the Boss 429 was a brilliant idea because it sped up production on the assembly line and lowered the cost. Unnecessary competition options were not offered because the goal was to get these engines into the cars and out the door as fast as possible. On the retail side, buyers were looking for performance,

An assembled Boss 429 engine shows the huge heads and oversized valvecovers. Installing this oversized engine in the smaller Mustang engine compartment presented a challenge. This is a fairly complete engine, built from NOS parts. This is an original Holley 735-carburetor for the Boss 429, which comes from the factory with a breather cap as shown. It has the original exhaust manifolds, the oil filter adapter that goes up to the oil cooler, and one of the oil pans.

not gingerbread, and they weren't disappointed. Right off the line, the car could turn a 0-100–mph time of 13.9-seconds. For those who wanted to dress up the cars, dealer options were available. The Kar-Kraft facility was ready to deliver the first Mustangs on January 15, 1969.

ASSEMBLY LINE PROGRAM

Bruce Guertin worked on the Ford factory assembly line from Jan 2, 1968, until September 7, 1970, and had a first-hand look at the Boss 429 assembly program. He was the shift roll-test driver in the Ford plant. At the end of the assembly line, the cars were driven to the front-end alignment station where the wheel toe-in was set and windshield wipers were installed. The cars then proceeded to one of four roller chassis dyno stations where they were tested for speedometer accuracy, steering function, transmission operation, electrical items, and fluid leaks. Guertin observed that the "Boss 429 had lots of leaks." This was due, in part, to the precise way that the cylinder heads had to be mounted and bolted onto the engine block. As mentioned earlier, these engines used the dry-deck rings and they did not use conventional head gaskets. Today, rebuilt Boss 429s are

In addition to overall engine width, weight was a consideration as was fitting the exhaust manifolds. This engine has an aftermarket air cleaner that draws more air than the factory snorkel. Factory air cleaners are very expensive to replace if they are stolen or damaged. Rated at 375-hp, these engines often produce 480 to 520 hp on the dyno. The drag-race engines can be pumped up to 1,100 to 1,200 hp in supercharged versions.

seen that leak if the dry-deck O-rings and seals were not installed correctly.

At the end of the factory assembly line, four roller stations tested the cars. Approximately 75 percent of the cars coming off the line were equipped with automatic transmissions, so three of the four roller stations were designated for the automatics; the remaining roller station was for manuals. Guertin's job was to drive the 17 cars per hour that were moved onto that roller station. He said, "This meant that I got to drive Boss 302s, 429s, and the 428CJs with, and without, the Drag Pak."

When the program began, all Boss 429s came down the line with a 428 installed. Bruce and his crew then test-drove them. After that, the cars went to Kar-Kraft

where the engine was changed out for the new Boss 429; then the cars returned to Dearborn Assembly. Back at the assembly plant, the cars were test-driven again, the Boss 429 fender sticker and window stickers were applied, and the finished cars were loaded onto the rail cars for delivery to the dealers.

In the middle of February 1969, which was after the first 100 or so cars, the Kar-Kraft facility ran out of room to store the removed 428 engines. Because of this, the cars that were to be transported to Kar-Kraft began rolling off the assembly line without engines. After the new Boss 429 engines were installed and the other modifications completed, the cars were returned to the factory for the final inspection.

These cars have just arrived and are heading down the line, ready for modification to begin. The hoods have not been removed, which signifies that the check-in process is not complete. (Photo Courtesy Ford Images)

Before the hood was separated from the car, the hood and the firewall were marked with corresponding numbers. In this case, the number is 11. Sub-assembly lines were set up parallel to the assembly line to speed up the conversion process; it also permitted greater inventory control. In this area, suspension parts, new spindles, and larger springs are being assembled. They will also add the new anti-sway bar. (Photo Courtesy Ford Images)

The next row over is the dress-up line where special components were installed on the engine and it was readied for installation. Having additional sub-assembly lines along the main assembly sped up production, and ensured tighter quality control. (Photo Courtesy Ford Images)

On the assembly line at Kar-Kraft, everything that could be unbolted from the firewall forward was removed. Next, the inner fender wells and shock tower mounts were cut loose from the front frame members. These needed to be moved out 1 inch on each side so that the enormous engine could fit in the engine bay. Ford later installed the shock towers at Ford Dearborn.

To create clearance for the block and the exhaust manifolds, the front suspension mounts had to be relocated. The front A-arms were lowered 1 inch and reinforced in preparation for the new engine.

The engine oil cooler was reinstalled at this time. It was attached using a bolt hole already in the core support that was intended for mounting the horn on the

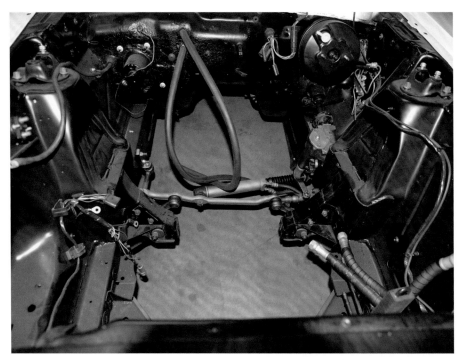

This 1969 Boss 429, KK number 1668, has 1,895 miles on it. Purchased in Idaho, the car has absolutely no rust. It had been raced and the only thing done was to strip off the paint because it had racing decals all over it. With all modifications completed, this engine bay is ready for installation of the new engine. Even after all this work is finished, it is still a very tight fit.

Engine mount bolts are in place. Note the angle of the shock tower and the additional bracing welded in place to handle the larger, heavier engine. Kar-Kraft made all of the visible spot welds and stitch welds.

The optional engine oil cooler was mounted in the hole where the driver-side horn would normally be installed. These coolers were standard on the Boss 429, and kept the oil at a safe operating temperature.

With the new oil cooler installed, a third hole was drilled and both horns were mounted on the passenger's side of the front support bar. Needless to say, numerous modifications were made to fit this whole package together.

The power steering cooler was installed in front of the engine, right behind the radiator. This is a necessary item that works very well in hot climates.

This very special master cylinder brake booster sits at an angle on the firewall. An aluminum piece underneath the booster and against the firewall positions the booster at an angle so it clears the valvecover. The instruction book states that when the brakes are bled, the back of the car must be jacked up 12 to 13 degrees to get the master cylinder level.

stock Mustangs. A hole was drilled on the other side and the horns mounted there. Because the horn was moved, a special wiring harness was created so that it would reach. This was only for the Boss 302 Drag Paks, Cobra Jet Drag Paks, and Boss 429 cars.

To gain more space in the engine compartment, the battery was moved to the passenger-side trunk, just behind the wheelwell. This necessitated using a space saver spare tire that was relocated to the driver's side of the trunk.

The original Autolite battery cable that runs all the way from the trunk is in the passenger's side of the engine compartment, and only on the Boss 429. As it goes down through the firewall, it curves out and then runs down though the rocker panel. At this point, it's covered with steel flexible conduit to prevent the cable from being cut and burning the car to the ground.

Even with modifications, the Boss 429 was a tight fit in the engine bay. However, with wider front suspension, the special Kar-Kraft wheel spindles, and lower control arms, the added performance and handling certainly made the effort worthwhile. These changes lowered the front of the car by 1 inch, just enough to improve front end geometry and handling.

While the hood was off the car during chassis modifications and engine installation, a large hole was

Ford had this wedge-shaped mount cast in aluminum. It's installed between the booster and the firewall to tilt the master cylinder up for the required clearance. (Photo Courtesy Ford Images)

The moment of truth is when the new engine is fitted into the modified engine bay. It took at least four people to fit the engine in place, with two above and two below. (Photo Courtesy Ford Images)

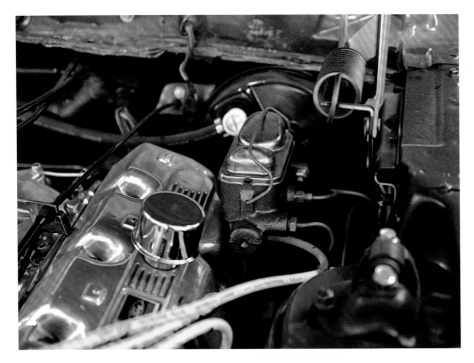

Even with the brake master cylinder angled upward, the clearance between it and the valvecover is minimal.

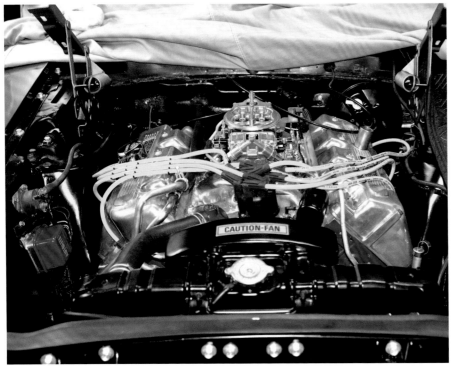

cut in the hood to allow installation of a large fiberglass air scoop to feed the air cleaner with the necessary air. When the hood is closed, the scoop becomes a functional manually operated ram air hood scoop. In 1969, the scoop was painted to match the color of the car. In 1970, the scoop was painted black.

Inside the Boss 429's front and rear fenders is a special rolled edge. The stock fenders have about a 3/4-inch lip inside, but it had to be rolled out of the way even more on the Boss 429 to make room for the larger tires. The edge starts out flat at the bottom and then is rolled in as it works its way up toward the center. The flared fenders are a telltale sign that identifies the vehicle as either a Boss 429 or a 302.

If the shop were in a hurry, hammer marks may be felt (as is true on KK 1668); this would have been unacceptable on some of the earlier cars. They simply beat the fenders out to miss the tires and moved the cars through production as early and quickly as they could. Toward

The engine fits with minimal clearance and is a tight fit all the way around the engine compartment. The Boss 429 engine fan cover is new.

After the engine was installed, the car went back onto the hoist; the exhaust was hooked up and the rear sway bar was mounted. (Photo Courtesy Ford Images)

The car is running on the rollers. It's being checked for vibration, tire balance and alignment, and any problems or adjustments that must be made. (Photo Courtesy Ford Images)

Final adjustments are made before the hood scoop is installed, and the car moves forward toward the quality control inspection area. (Photo Courtesy Ford Images)

Another clue to the vehicle's identity was the enormous hood scoop. The opening at the front of the scoop could be opened or closed by a cable control located under the driver's side dashboard. In effect, it was similar to a manual choke. On a cold morning, the scoop was closed, and after the engine warmed up, the scoop was opened for maximum air intake.

The inner fenderwells were rolled more to make room for the larger tires. Otherwise, they would rub under acceleration and cornering.

The only outside marking on the Boss 429 that identified what was under the hood was the lettering on the front fenders of the finished cars.

QUALITY CONTRO

FINAL INSPECTION

AREA

At the final inspection area for quality control, the car received its last once-over before the factory released it for final drive-out and another inspection before being shipped. (Photo Courtesy Ford Images)

The first Boss 429 Mustang arrives at the end of the assembly line at the Kar-Kraft facility. The windshield wipers have been installed, but the Boss lettering hasn't been applied to the front fenders. Roy Lunn (left) was the project officer and Fran Hernandez (right) was the manufacturing manager. (Photo Courtesy Ford Images)

Quality control was very important for this project. Inspections were ongoing as the cars went down the line. This is one of the inspection sheets that were left under the back seat of KK 1279.

the end of the production run, when they got down to crunch time, some of the cars went out without even having the fenders rolled. Kar-Kraft was pumping the cars out at a rate of about 10 per day to meet the quota.

Kar-Kraft placed the original build sheet, two inspection sheets, and a reject or redo sheet underneath the back seat. Over the years, these were often removed. When Boss 429 owner Denny Aldridge removed the back seat on his car, he found these very rare papers.

The sheets that Aldridge found are all marked NASCAR or special NASCAR, etc. Underneath the seats was an underlayment, or "sound deadener" that is like tarpaper, which is, of course, a petroleum. The sheets sat on the paper and through the years the paper sucked up the oil, so most of them are stained and look dark or oily.

There is a big difference between the early and late battery tray supports. These were actually spot welded to the floor pan. When the Boss 429 engine was installed in the car, the battery was moved from the engine compartment to the passenger-side rear corner in the trunk. This was partly due to lack of space in the engine bay and also to aid in traction. When customers ordered replacement parts, confusion often arose because many didn't realize that there was a difference in the mounting plates.

The car listed on this reject sheet had a problem with its paint and had to be redone. This is part of the car's history and obviously goes with it. Denny Aldridge found this sheet underneath the rear seat when it was disassembled.

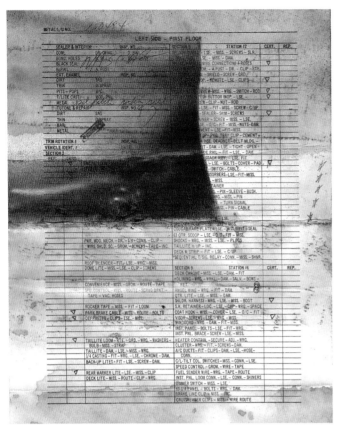

Another car in the Aldridge collection is a Wimbledon White Boss 429, KK 1668. It has a later battery box mount that is shaped differently. There is no record of serial numbers noting when Ford went from one mount to the other. I think that the first 50 to 100 cars are like the red car; then the change was made and the rest are more like the later cars.

This reject sheet is extremely rare because it has the serial number of the car and NASCAR written on it. The little stamping of the inspector is still visible.

A red 1969 Boss 429, KK 1279, an early production car, is in the Aldridge collection. It was sold and transported by a convoy truck to Organ Ford in Compton, California. Upon arrival, the driver fired the car up and backed it off his convoy truck. The driver knew that it was a specialty car; he left it idling and ran inside to ask where he should park it. When he went back outside, the car was gone. Two months later, it was recovered from under a Los Angeles freeway. It had 10.5 miles on the odometer and was like new except that the engine and transmission were missing. The insurance company covered the loss and the car stayed on the back of the dealer's lot under a tarp until it was sold in 1972 for $1,200. In 1974, with the same mileage, it was sold for $1,000. The car has been part of the Aldridge collection for the past 43 years with current mileage of less than 3,000 miles. The engine and transmission were never recovered. This wasn't a big deal because Aldridge Motorsports specializes in building Boss 429 engines and transmissions.

Because this is an early car, the battery tray support is cut off at the front and there's a step-out to miss the original tie-down strap for the spare tire. The mini spare was moved to the opposite side where there's a protector to miss the taillight for the space saver spare.

This is a unique battery tray designed specifically for the Boss 429. It bolts on top of the battery box mount in the trunk. Kar-Kraft wanted to use the biggest battery possible. They were mounting the battery in the passenger-side rear corner of the trunk, and as such, cables had to run from the front of the car to the back.

This has the 3/4-inch-under rear-end sway bar, a unique piece for the Boss 429 only. The square mounts on the solid rear axle that mount the sway bar are called dog bones. The 1970 model had a different sway bar installed.

All Boss 429 cars had drum brakes on the rear. In addition, they came with the Autolite rear shock absorbers with bearing special KK part numbers.

This car sat in storage for about 30 years. When it was time to bring it out and make it roadworthy, the mufflers and rear section of the exhaust pipes needed replacing.

The transmission crossmember mount was designed for the original 428 Cobra Jet engine. Ford added a slotted piece to the front of the transmission mount so it would line up and bolt in correctly.

Concerned with voltage and amperage drop, the Boss 429 team sourced the biggest battery and mounting tray they could find from Ford Truck Division: the Group 29 battery. The Group 29 batteries and trays are no longer available, so restorers of these cars use a Group 27 batteries and trays. There is little size difference between the two. The Group 27 battery measures 12 x 6¾ x 9 inches high at the top of the post. The Group 29 battery measures 12 x 5½ x 9 inches. The reproduction batteries come with the original red caps. The Group 27 batteries are only about $285.

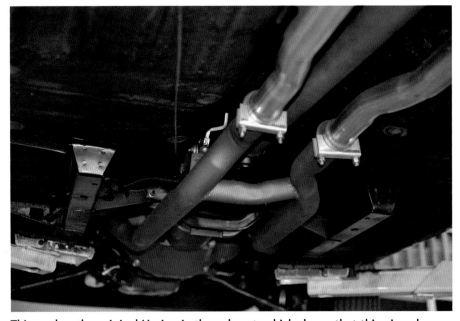

This car has the original H-pipe in the exhaust, which shows that this piece has not been replaced. This part is unique to the Boss 429.

Ford engineers felt that because 80 percent of the stopping was courtesy of the front brakes, discs were used. The rear brakes handled the remaining 20 percent. Therefore, the rear was still fitted with drum brakes, which were more abundant as well as being cheaper to produce and install.

SUSPENSION

Ford retained the duties for developing the Boss 302 suspension in-house, but Kar-Kraft was responsible for revising the Boss 429 suspension and finding a way to shoehorn the engine between the shock towers.

Similar to other Mustangs, the Boss 429 was fitted with a double A-arm front suspension with the lower A-arm positioning the spring. From the get-go, Kar-Kraft had a lot of fabricating to do to get the Boss 429 to fit into the standard fastback

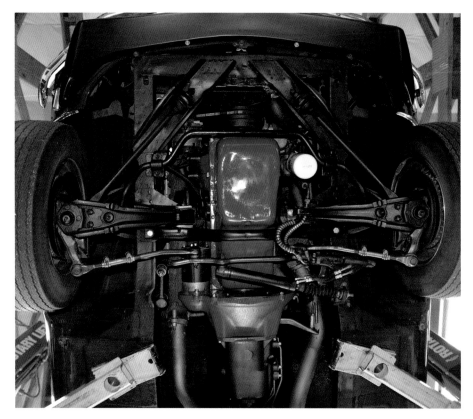

By looking straight at the front end, it is easy to see the wider stance where the shock towers were moved to make room for the big aluminum heads. When they moved the suspension, they changed all of the pivot points on the A-arms to try to keep the geometry correct. The spindle has a KK part number; it was a Kar-Kraft–only spindle. Its diameter is greater and it has bigger bearings because this engine was very heavy. This alteration also improved the handling, although that wasn't the original intent.

body. In fact, the Boss 429 was 2 inches too wide for the shock towers, which were the narrowest point in the engine bay. To accommodate the behemoth engine, each shock tower was trimmed and pushed out 1 inch on each side. As a result, Kar-Kraft had to rework most of the suspension parts, which included revised shock towers, shock tower brace, new upper control arms, heavy-duty springs, and heavy-duty uprights. However, the modifications didn't stop there. A smaller brake booster was installed that didn't contact the valvecover. In addition, Ford installed 60-series tires that were large for the time and therefore required extra space. The larger engine, as well as the increased tire size, necessitated re-engineering the suspension. Everything on the 1969 Boss 429 front suspension is unique except for the lower control arms.

REAR SUSPENSION

Like other Mustangs of the day, the Boss 429 was equipped with a live axle, multi-leaf rear suspension. However, it differed from other Boss 429s because the springs were heavy duty with a thicker 5/8-inch anti-roll bar. In addition, the rear suspension received staggered shocks to increase traction and help prevent wheel hop.

This car has the original rear sway bar and the original 9-inch Ford nodular rear end. As you know, the Boss

This is the strut rod. The scratches and dings are clearly visible. It was common for people to roll a floor jack under the car and either try to jack it up on the crossmember or on the strut rod, which bent.

Everything in the front end was engineered very closely. The power steering was engineered to fit, but not hit the pan or the bellhousing.

429 arrived standard with a nodular case and 31-spline axles that featured a 3.9:1 Trac-Lok rear end.

These solid-rear-axle cars used staggered shock absorbers to increase stability, help control wheel hop, and aid in traction. Keep in mind that the Boss 429s were actually Mustang Cobra Jets as they moved down the assembly line, so the staggered shock and 4-speed transmission configuration was standard for the higher-performance Mustangs.

This car's driveshaft is an unusual length because the engine is mounted farther forward in the car because of the large head size. Therefore, when the Boss engine was moved forward, the transmission mount had to be modified to make everything line up.

Because the front suspension was widened, the front tracking was also. Suspension perches were relocated, new spindles were fabricated, and the ride height was lowered. Even though it wasn't designed for cornering, the Boss 429 offered dramatically improved road manners compared to the Mach 1s. The strut arm braces extend from the frame to the front of the crossmember. The startup strut arm locates itself to keep the lower A-arm from folding back when the brakes are applied.

WHEELS

"The Magnum 500 Boss 429 wheel has a very similar cap to the Chrysler Magnum 500, which is commonly called the 2-inch cap," according to Denny Aldridge. "It is a tapered cap that has a running horse decal in the center, and if you peel that back, it wasn't unheard of to find the crossed-flag Magnum 500 Chrysler decal underneath."

Something else unique about these wheels is that they have the number and date code stamped on the inside of the wheel. Only the Boss 429 Magnum wheel had chrome spokes; the spokes on the Boss 302 and other cars had a satin finish. The Boss 429 used a very specific wheel and tire combination.

This car has the original Magnum 15 x 7 wheels. However, it sat for a long time and the tires were in bad shape, so original tires and wheels from another Boss 429 were located. The tires and wheels are original equipment and correct for this car.

"Dyno Don" Nicholson received one of the two Mercury Cougars that were fitted with the Boss 429 engine. He didn't use it for very long; instead he opted for the Cammer engine. The original engine sits beside the car. The middle car is Al Joniec's Boss 429 Pro Stock car that is now owned by Joe Spinelli.

The Boss 429 was squarely focused on NASCAR competition even though it would be used for drag racing. For years, Holman-Moody was the official racing contractor for Ford and had been involved in NASCAR racing for decades. As such, it was fully prepared to support and service the Boss 429 program.

In early 1956, John Holman arrived in Charlotte, North Carolina, and took over Ford's NASCAR program. This came about after it became clear that Ford was getting off the racetracks, and a private contractor whose only business was racing could do the job better and more efficiently. John Holman and Ralph Moody formed the Holman-Moody partnership in 1957.

Then they went to talk to Ford. After some negotiation, Ford accepted their $12,000 bid to buy all of Ford's surplus race equipment. The company expanded rapidly and relocated onto the grounds of the Charlotte-Douglas Airport. Four buildings provided space for fabrication, engine building, preparation, and storage. The company grew to provide major parts sales and production. In the early 1970s, Holman-Moody stocked almost everything related to the Boss 429.

Every imaginable part for serious racing was available over the counter. It also stockpiled obsolete original Boss 429 Mustang parts as Ford discontinued them. Keep in mind, Ford was no longer producing the Boss

This rare valvecover was available on the first 200 cars. They were just like the regular Boss 429 valvecovers except that they were magnesium, to lighten the car. This particular set of valvecovers was on a NASCAR vehicle; you can tell by the dual breather setup.

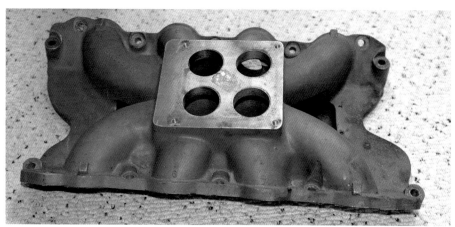

Ford, along with Holman-Moody, originally designed this blue spider manifold for use on the shorter tracks. What makes this manifold special is that the flange where the carburetor bolts on is a larger area than other manifolds. This allows the carburetor to be moved around on the manifold to obtain maximum air and fuel distribution.

The removable bottom allowed cleaning of the underside of the manifold, and kept the hot oil from hitting the bottom of the manifold.

Smokey Yunick's intake manifolds had some very unusual and unique numbers.

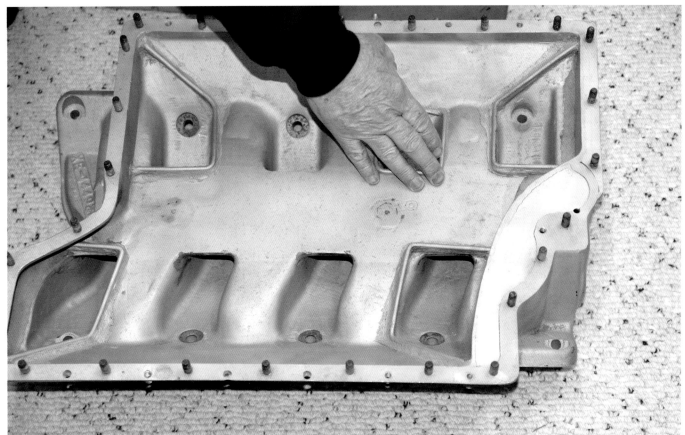

The bottom bolts on the later intake manifolds were safety wired so they couldn't fall out.

1969–1970 Ford Mustang Boss 429
In Detail No. 7

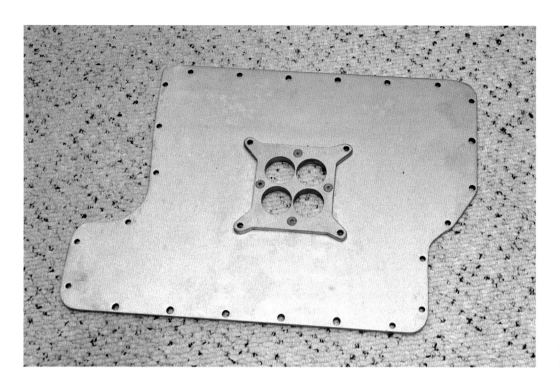

This D-shaped manifold plate has the center square-bore intake.

429 and wasn't looking back, so Holman-Moody picked up all the inventory it could get and made it available to the general public, especially the racing crowd.

Because it was performance-driven, Holman-Moody knew the good old boy NASCAR crowd. And it knew how to build winning cars. It supplied Ford and Mercury cars to many winning stock car teams. It was the first to develop a dedicated stock car chassis; it also introduced the roll cage and driver seat support.

Holman-Moody prepared the GT-40 MkIIs, A/FX Mustangs, Shelby Cobras, Falcons, and of course, stock cars. It was heavily involved in the Boss 429 preparation for NASCAR. In addition, it modified and created its own Boss 429 engine parts, which included intake manifolds, exhaust manifolds, and a wide variety of high-performance parts. When Ford was no longer fielding or supporting the Boss 429 project, Holman-Moody sold its excess parts to several companies with an interest in these cars and engines, including Aldridge Motorsports.

ENGINE DEVELOPMENT

In 2015, Ford Performance Public Relations interviewed NASCAR Hall of Fame Nominee, Robert Yates, about his work on the Boss 429. Yates started working at Holman-Moody in 1967 shortly after Ford won the 24 Hours of Le Mans for the second straight year. His main responsibility at the time was to prep parts and have them ready for the 30 engine builders on staff. A couple of years later, he became part of a group that was challenged to develop and prepare the Boss 429 for NASCAR competition. During an interview, he stated that Ford wanted a hemispherical engine like Chrysler's, but it wanted a better engine. He felt that they had done a good job. "We got the engines from Ford, and the first runs were really about 580 hp, which is what the tunnel ports were making," he said.

The Holman-Moody crew started with the cylinder heads, making the ports much smaller and doing a lot of flow work. They fabricated their own pistons with longer

Smokey Yunick worked on many experimental engines and race projects throughout his career. One of those involved a set of heads that came from his shop when the Boss 429 items were sold. It's a set of cylinder heads with a lot of numbers on them, either from Smokey or from Ford Engineering. Denny Aldridge now owns the heads.

It looks like they were designed for a standard-size head gasket, because no O-rings are cut in the heads. They could have been designed to run with a NASCAR block, for which the O-ring was in the block itself. The flowcharts are stamped on the exhaust side, or these numbers could be the cubic-centimeter measurement of the runners. Smokey probably had his own way of listing this stuff, but you can see that the numbers are very close from one exhaust port to the other.

Also unusual is that on the under side of the head are some drilled and tapped spots that look like an area for a spring. Back then, they used something called a rev kit that consisted of an extra valvespring to help control the lifter stay on the camshaft. This worked on the pushrod side because it had more leverage to better control the lifter. Very few of these sets were made, probably less than a handful.

In 1970, while working for Ford, Smokey built a variable-length intake runner for the 302 engine used in Trans-Am racing and the Boss 429. His plan was for a cross-ram arrangement in which three sides of the runner remained full-length, but the top of the runner had a vacuum-controlled, gear-activated retractable runner roof. It showed remarkable potential. As RPM increased, runners became shorter because negative pressure dropped at high RPM.

Another Smokey Yunick manifold was built called a rat roaster.

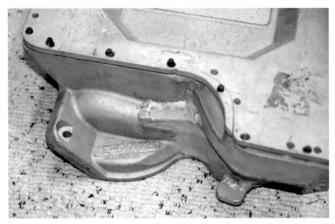

Holman-Moody produced this glass-beaded silver intake manifold specifically for NASCAR-prepared engines, as indicated by the SK and XH markings.

Under the head is a drilled and tapped area and what looks like a place where a spring would fit. When these cars were new, rev kits were occasionally available. The kit contained an extra valvespring to help control the lifter stay on the camshaft. Positioning it on the side of the pushrod gave it more leverage to control the lifter. Very few of these sets made.

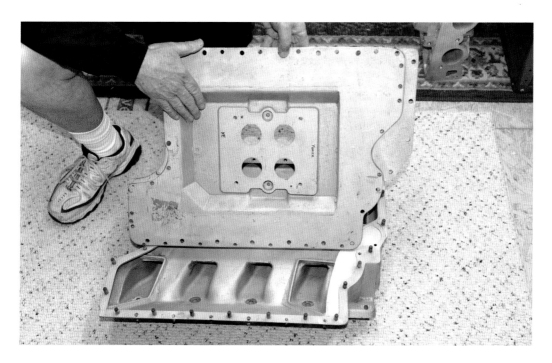

This rare manifold is from the Smokey Yunick collection. Many people call them rat roasters, because of the unusual plenum and design. The configuration of the ports is completely different, as is the height of the carburetor. Smokey was always trying something different, and many times he was spot on.

connecting rods, producing an output of 620 hp. Keep in mind that that was with a dry sump. "It was one of the nicest laid out engines I've ever seen to this day," he went on to say. By changing the ports and tuning the engine, they were able to extract 610 to 620 hp. There was a big push to get these engines finished, in the cars, and on the track, so the crews were working up to 100 hours a week through 1969.

One of the biggest challenges faced was that the first connecting rods used broke the caps. First, they were breaking bolts, and then when stronger bolts were used, the caps broke. A lot of time and effort went into finding and correcting the problem.

By the time they were through, the crew was able to find an additional 50 hp when modifying and developing the Boss 429. The feeling at Holman-Moody was that they couldn't bring out the Boss 429 engine with the same numbers as the Chrysler tunnel port. This was because they knew that the Chrysler Hemi engines were probably making 590 or close to 600 hp, but when they came out with the finished Boss 429, "We kicked their

butt. We beat them in power. We beat them in weight. That engine was probably at least 100 pounds lighter. The Hemi was probably 700 pounds and the Boss was 600, so they paid attention to weight. They had magnesium oil pans on it and it was still an iron block, but it was well designed. It was a beautiful engine and the thing we wanted to do more than anything was beat the Chrysler."

At about the same time, Ford contracted Smokey Yunick to build the Boss 429 for racing applications. His driver was Swede Savage. The car was a 1970 Ford Torino Talladega with a Boss 429 in it with "about 640 horses, and about 200 pounds too much on the front wheels." Smokey went on to say that Swede did his part, "but my engine exploded 'bout 130 laps before the race was over."

The cars were now approaching 200 mph, so NASCAR decreed that after 1969, the engine limit was 430 ci. This meant that the manufacturers had to find the speed to win elsewhere, so they redesigned the cars. This was the period of NASCAR's aero wars. Dodge came out with a Charger 500 and later added

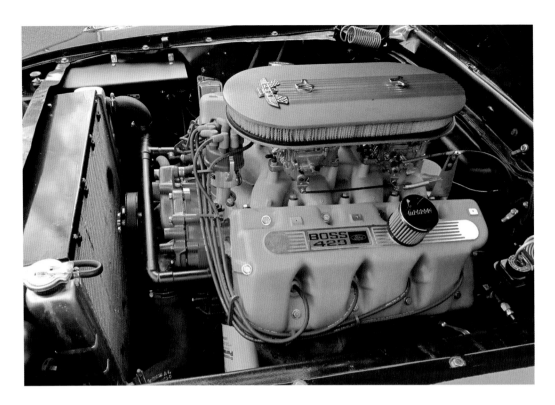

This resto rod is a highly modified KK-numbered car. Without the shock towers, there is plenty of room for the oversized heads on this Boss 429 with dual 4s.

the winged Charger Daytona. In 1970, the Plymouth Road Runner Super Bird had the aerodynamic front end and the high wing; hardly something you would drive on the street.

Struggling to stay competitive, Holman-Moody constructed a special front end for the Ford Torino that was longer and more aerodynamic. It was called the Talladega because it was designed for the high-bank, super-fast speedways. The Ford Torino Talladega was produced during the first few weeks of 1969. It helped make Ford even more competitive in NASCAR. The Mercury equivalent was called the Cyclone Spoiler II.

Before NASCAR would allow the Ford Torino Talladega's new design on the circuit, Ford had to roll at least 100 cars with this design off the assembly line. The only way to accomplish this was to have Holman-Moody fabricate the fenders and front ends during the week. Then, they delivered the parts to Ford's Atlanta plant and installed them on the weekends when the regular crew was not working. Some questions remain today as to whether or not 100 cars were actually built.

TOTAL PERFORMANCE

While under contract with Ford, Smokey Yunick built a Boss 429 that raced in the 1969 Pikes Peak Hill Climb and won with Bobby Unser behind the wheel. The engine is on display at The Speedway Motors Museum of American Speed in Lincoln, Nebraska.

During that period, the man in charge of the Total Performance Drag Racing Program for Ford was Dick Brannan. Back in the 1960s, Richard "Dick" Brannan was a successful independent drag racer who just happened to run a 1962 Ford Galaxie with a 406-ci Thunderbird Special V-8 engine rated at 405 hp.

Coming from out of town, he won the top award at the Detroit Dragway. This was the first time a Ford had taken the honors at that strip. "It was a great car. I'd been racing around my area and winning, which was unusual for a Ford at the time because it was the underdog."

It turned out to be a great evening with Brannan winning the race, beating a 409 Chevrolet in the finals. The brass at Ford sat up and took notice. Several days later, Brannan received a call from Dave Evans, manager of Ford's special vehicles program, inviting him to Dearborn. Brannan went and was later offered a position in the stock vehicles department where performance development was conducted.

It was there that they designed, developed, and launched the racing car programs. Initially, that included IndyCar engine research and development. That program was eventually transferred to another office, leaving Brannan's department with the Grand National (NASCAR), Drag Racing, and Le Mans development programs.

Right out of the box, the Boss 429 started winning races. Ford was rewarded with first- and second-place finishes in the Atlanta 500 on March 30, 1969. Holman-Moody built and supplied the engines for the Ford and Mercury NASCAR teams with great success. Ford Torino driver David Pearson took the season championship as well. By the end of the 1969 season, The Boss 429 engine had won 26 races, and other automobile manufacturers began to complain.

The engine was also very successful on the shorter tracks. Of the nine races that fell into this category, Ford won seven of them. By the end of the 1969 season, everyone in the Ford and Mercury camps was smiling. They finally had an engine and car combination that could compete on a level playing field.

Jacque Passino, Ford special vehicles manager, was elated. "With only one year under our belt, the Boss 429 already has surpassed our early expectations," he said. "We think it will establish itself as the most powerful and reliable race engine ever produced." Little did he know.

Unfortunately, the noise and complaints in the other camps grew loud enough that Bill France called a meeting to discuss the future of NASCAR and how it would play out with the major automobile manufacturers. By the end of 1970, with speeds approaching 200 mph, Bill France was concerned, and perhaps rightly so. In an effort to level the playing field, NASCAR officials required that certain engines, including the Boss 429, be run with restrictor plates between the carburetor and the intake manifold.

This reduced the air/fuel mixture getting through to the big-port heads and therefore curbed the horsepower. It wasn't long before the Ford teams were going from the Boss 429 to the 427 Wedge, depending on the track. Nevertheless, even with the restrictor plate, the Boss 429 was still winning races, just not as many.

In any racing endeavor, especially NASCAR, remaining competitive requires a well-funded organization fully behind the effort. When Ford pulled out of racing in 1971, it was the beginning of the end for the Boss 429.

The opinion was that the Boss 429 was a bit much and not in the spirit of NASCAR. One of the best engines ever designed and built had been regulated out of the competition by the end of 1970.

DRAG RACING

With Fran "the Man from Mercury" Hernandez, involved in the Boss 429 project, it should come as no surprise that Kar-Kraft built two Boss 429 Mercury Cougars. Ford created a special Cougar NASCAR package (DS0 84–8018) to authorize the build. The Lincoln-Mercury drag program, created specifically for Mercury drag team racers, immediately jumped onboard.

One Cougar went to "Fast Eddie" Schartman and the other to "Dyno Don" Nicholson. Both had the same trim package; white exterior with black interior and both featured fiberglass front fenders. Because the Cougar was the same size as the Mustang, these cars went down the line and received the same engine bay modifications as the Boss Mustangs. As it turned out, the cars had to be heavily modified after going to the race teams so that they were competitive in the Super Stock class.

Unfortunately, the Boss 429 Cougar build did not work out for the Lincoln-Mercury race teams. This engine was designed for NASCAR, not the quarter-mile, and the cars were too slow to be in the money. Nicholson quickly switched out his factory Boss engine for Ford's single overhead camshaft 427-ci V-8 (Cammer) engine. This high-output engine produced approximately 615 hp and 515 ft-lbs of torque.

Neither racer kept the cars for very long; they just weren't competitive. "Fast Eddie" Schartman used his Cougar to teach tuning at drag racing clinics. The agreement with Ford was that when they were finished, both cars would return to Ford. That never happened; but by then, Ford was no longer interested.

Neither car set the quarter-mile on fire and without the Kar-Kraft designation there was very little interest in them for decades after their retirement. When the Boss 429 Mustangs started to climb in value, the Cougars were tracked down and brought in for restoration. Today, only Dyno Don's car is restored and ready for display. Restoration work is underway on "Fast Eddie" Schartman's car.

Although developed primarily for NASCAR, the Boss 429 found its way onto the Can-Am tracks and into the frame rails of altered Mustangs and funny cars . . . and they won!

Probably the most famous drag racer to run a Boss 429 engine was "Ohio George" Montgomery. Ohio George was a longtime drag racer and was very good at it. Running primarily GM engines in a 1933 Willys, he dominated the sport for years. During my interview, Ohio George stated that Ford contacted him in the mid-1960s. "It wanted me to run a couple of its engines, primarily the 289," he said. "But I was doing quite well with the GM products, and I really wasn't interested."

He went on to say that he lost in the 1965 nationals, and soon after that, he called Ford. However, he didn't want the 289 engine, he wanted the exotic 427-ci SOHC engine, the Cammer. This engine was difficult to come by, but Ford wanted Ohio George on its team, so Donald Fry, one of the project planners on the original Mustang, found the necessary parts to build one. Ohio George started running the Ford 427 Cammer engine, but Ford still wasn't satisfied because it was a Willys-bodied car.

"One of the problems with running the Ford car was that it didn't have a frame, it was unibody construction," said Ohio George. "So after consulting with NHRA, we built a 1933 Willys frame and put a fiberglass Mustang body over it and ran the first one in 1967."

In 1969, Ford decided to upgrade the Mustang and use a new Mach 1 body with a Boss 429 engine. The original idea was to run a 671 GMC supercharger, but that didn't work out very well, "The engine was designed for the track, not for drag racing," he said. Next came the twin turbo project. Unfortunately, just about the time that Ohio George had the twin turbo Boss 429 engine built and running, Ford pulled out of the racing program.

Using his own money, Ohio George went ahead and finished the project. He ran the car successfully, which was known as the *Mr. Gasket Gasser*. After winning the 1973 and 1974 Gator Nationals, he retired the car. Ohio George retired from drag racing altogether at the age of 53. He is now 84 years and, with his son, continues to run his own speed and machine shop.

This was the end of the era. The privateers and grassroots racers took the ball and ran with it, but without big corporate sponsorship, the Boss 429 became too expensive to run. It was just a matter of time until it was shoved to the back of the garage, in favor of engines such as the Wedge, which was easier to maintain and cheaper to build. Although its time may have been short, it made a real impact on the racetrack and at the drags.

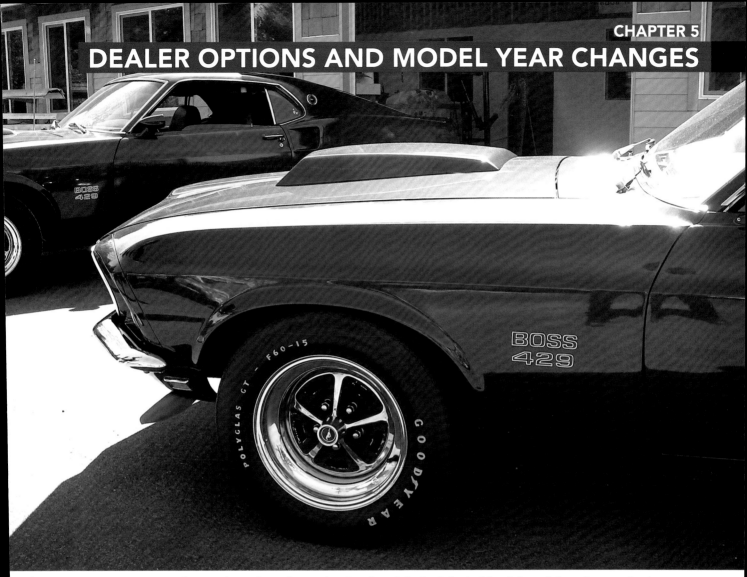

The 1969 Mustang Boss 429 featured simple and restrained styling; it lacked the bold striping of the other production Mustangs. The only clue as to what was under the hood was the outline lettering on the side and the oversized hood scoop.

When the Boss 429 Mustangs came off the assembly line no factory optional accessories were available. The focus was getting the first 500 cars (engines) into the hands of the public as soon as possible.

Because the Boss 429 Mustang was more about an engine than an entire vehicle, its exterior makeover was relatively simple. The flash normally associated with the Mustang was purposely deleted. This was a new sleeper in the Mustang stable for 1969. The Mustang's quarter panel air scoop did not route cool air to the rear brakes; it was purely for styling. The running horse emblems on the upper rear quarter panels stayed. The distinctive identifying trademark for the Boss was the square, functional air scoop bolted to the top the hood. This was the biggest hood scoop that Ford ever produced.

FUNCTIONAL HOOD SCOOP

The functional hood scoop was standard equipment on both model years and was extremely popular with buyers. Being able to open or close the scoop from the inside of the car was a big deal in 1969. On cold mornings, the scoop could be left closed until the engine was adequately warmed up. Then, it could be opened partially or all the way, depending on driving conditions and performance options.

The new Mustang body style for 1969 featured four headlights. They were staggered with the outside two recessed into the fenders. The two inner headlights were set up so that they could be exchanged for high-speed driving lights.

1969–1970 Ford Mustang Boss 429
In Detail No. 7

The rear wing and door stripes that were so popular on the earlier Mustangs were no longer part of the design for the Boss 429. The only things on the austere sides of the car were the large outline letters BOSS and 429 located on the front fenders, just behind the wheelwells. The front spoiler was standard, but was shipped in the trunk and installed at the dealership. The Boss 429 Mustangs were so low in the front that the car haulers, or transporters, were tearing them off when loading the cars on the transport trailers.

In 1969, the retail base price for a Boss 429 Mustang was a mere $4,740. That didn't leave much markup or profit for the dealer. The Boss 429 didn't feature ostentatious styling treatments; rather, the styling was very clean, conservative, and purposeful. While considerable resources were dedicated to developing the Boss 429 engine, the cars also carried many premium features, such as Deluxe interior, competition suspension, Magnum 500 wheels, and more.

After the cars arrived at the dealership, it was a different story. Dealerships make their profit by selling and installing accessories; they were anxious to dress up these plain cars and add to their bottom line.

By the time the cars were offered to the customer, it was not uncommon to see them decked out with sports slats on the rear windows, a trunk spoiler, fold-down rear seat, vinyl trim stripes, a custom floor shifter, (such as Hurst), and whatever else would pump up the bottom line. (The Hurst shifter was available from the Ford dealers as an option in 1969; it was standard equipment in 1970.)

ACCESSORIES AND OPTIONS

Here are some popular options for the 1969 Boss 429. Italian engineers for the Ferrari and Lamborghini sports cars originally designed the sport slats, or European louvers, as they were known. They showed up in Italy in the 1960s, and it wasn't long before they were an option on the new Mustangs. This option was a very popular accessory because they covered the big rear window; they kept the sunlight out and looked cool without hindering rear visibility.

Thanks to Carroll Shelby, a new wood-grain steering wheel was high on the list of cool things to have. A simulated woodgrain steering wheel was standard on all 1969 Boss 9s. These came out of the European sports cars and were marketed by Shelby. They were standard on all Shelby Mustangs, so it wasn't long before these great looking steering wheels showed up on a lot of Mustangs. They became standard on the Boss 429.

Bigger wheels and larger tires for better traction were also popular. Both Firestone and Goodyear were dealer-connected; the cars could arrive at the dealership, be fitted with new rubber and fancy wheels, and then the customer paid the bill at the dealership.

The rear spoiler (or wing), a dealer option, was offered mid-year 1969 on the Boss 302s. It was available with all required hardware to retrofit it to the Boss 429.

I think it's safe to say that most Mustang owners appreciate a good sound system. However, the Boss 429 was a specialty-built competition-oriented car, and as such, it did have some spartan appointments. An AM radio was the only one available for the Boss 429, so those who wanted the best purchased two matching kick panel speakers to go with a new upscale radio.

Holley carburetors had been part of performance and racing for a long time. Holley developed a wide variety of carburetors and a 735-cfm unit was fitted to the Boss 429. At that time, any local engine shop could handle the installation and tuning.

In 1970, Ford dealers began offering GT fog lights that included brackets, a wiring harness, switches, and bulbs. These were a real step up because the cars could easily outdrive the stock headlights. These new GT lights were also available as off-road driving lights that provided far more visibility than the stock units.

Traction Master underride traction bars were considered almost a necessity for the Boss 429s when using the cars for drag racing. The 1969 and 1970 Boss 429s had leaf spring rear suspension, common for the day,

The rear window slats, or louvers, were a popular option. Designed to break up the large rear window space, they also shielded the interior from the sun, which helped keep the interior cooler.

1969–1970 Ford Mustang Boss 429
In Detail No. 7

Custom Carroll Shelby–style steering wheels were often used to dress up the interior. They were available with leather-covered rims and any logo desired on the center horn cap.

The Boss 429 interior contained rich woodgrain accents and soft bucket seats, so it wasn't a hard sell to upgrade to rear fold-down seats. This allowed access to the trunk from the inside and also allowed the loading of boxes or items that were too large or too long for the trunk.

The classic lines of the 1969 fastback shared with the Boss 429 endure in the current line of Mustang cars. This particular 1969 model carries Sport Slats, rear spoiler, and Magnum 500 wheels.

88

During the muscle car era, Boss 429s were modified for drag racing and other forms of competition. They were so rare and valuable that few were built into resto-mod machines, so this particular example is even rarer. This exterior view does not hint at the aftermarket parts under the skin.

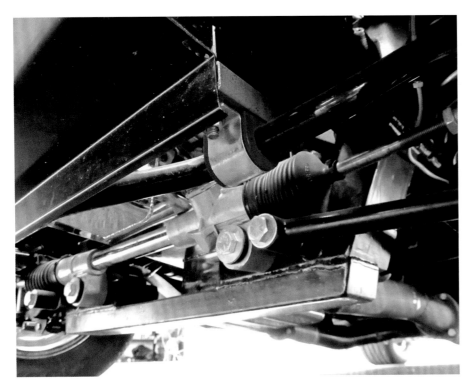

With this resto mod, the front shock towers were removed and a complete power rack-and-pinion steering was installed. Not only is the steering much more precise, but there is now much more room in the engine bay.

Inside the resto mod, the floor rails were reinforced and a roll bar was installed. The upright supports are hidden in the walls. Note that the top of the shoulder belt is bolted to the roll bar for additional safety.

This Boss 429 carries the alluring Black Jade color. The massive functional hood scoop graces the hood. Although the chin spoiler appeared similar to the Boss 302, it was in fact shallower.

The quarter panel brake scoops were for adornment and were not functional. The front spoiler and the massive hood scoop were unique to the Boss 429.

which tramped under hard acceleration. The springs tended to wind up and twist, resulting in wheel hop. Carroll Shelby was one of the first racers and performance car builders to tout the addition of Traction Master bars and he installed them on all of his GT 350s. The same traction bars were available through the local Ford dealer and were a bolt-on item for the Boss 429.

In addition to the traction bars, performance shock absorbers were also a necessity for anyone racing these cars. The competition shocks were heavier duty and adjustable. The solid axle rear ends benefited greatly from the heavier shock absorbers, in addition to the traction bar.

A variety of custom side mirrors were available as accessories, so if you didn't like the original mirrors, you had options. Shelby had a set of his own, called bullet mirrors, as well as dual racing mirrors. The 1969–1970 Boss 429 carried racing mirrors as standard equipment. Another interesting option was a remote-controlled deluxe mirror on the driver's side.

The 1969 and 1970 Mustang had three taillights on each side, as did the Mercury. So it wasn't very long before dealers were selling an installation kit for sequential taillights. This was an easy installation and the effect at night was impressive.

The 1969 Boss 429 featured one muffler that was mounted in front of and perpendicular to the differential; the 1970 Boss 429 was fitted with two inline mufflers. Those looking for more power purchased free-flowing mufflers that were available from a variety of dealers. The Ford dealership's body shop would make the exchange.

Fender flares on the rear fender wheel lips, which allowed larger rear tires, were a popular body modification for amateur drag racers. Some dealerships had equipment in their body and fender shops to perform this and other modifications.

A number of Boss 429s wound up in recycling and scrap yards and were parted out for a fraction of their value. Some owners removed the Boss 429 engine and replaced it with a street 429-ci engine. Several owners even turned their stock Boss 429 Mustangs into drag cars or resto mods. Because of the extreme torque and horsepower that the engine could produce, some engines were removed from the cars for use in other applications, such as tractor pulling.

A resto mod car has the outside appearance of the original, but the outdated parts, such as engine, drivetrain, suspension, wiring, and interior, are replaced with more-modern high-performance parts. The purists shudder at the thought of modifying an original classic such as the Boss Mustang.

Surprisingly enough, a number of Boss 429 resto mods have sold for more than $200,000.

No one knows for sure how many original cars have survived. Now that they have become so popular and command such a high price, more and more cars are being pulled out of the barns and back alleys to be restored. A few clones have appeared on the market, some of which are almost perfect copies.

In addition, an attempt has been made to reunite some of the surviving cars with their correct Boss 429 engines.

MODEL YEAR CHANGES

The Boss 429 Mustangs were only built in 1969 and 1970. The Mustang body style was all new for 1969. It featured quad headlights up front, with the outer tubing more recessed and mounted in the outside edge of the fenders. The two inner lights were mounted on the grille, as Carroll Shelby had done with his Shelby Mustangs.

The 1969 model was also larger and wider than previous Mustangs. It was considered a more aggressive design and sales predictions for the model year were high. All models of the 1969 Mustang sold very well, except for the Boss 429, which, of course, was not designed for the public. Going into the 1970 model year, dealers still had unsold previous-year cars on the lot.

In 1969, Ford/Kar-Kraft produced 859 Boss 429s, including the two Cougars for Lincoln/Mercury Race Division. The much-talked-about hood scoop was the same color as the car. All Boss 429s came with the

The front end on the 1970 model has two headlights instead of the four of the previous year. The outside two were replaced with front-brake air vents that are nonfunctional. Many felt that this was a cleaner, smoother design than the 1969 model.

The taillights on the 1970 Boss 429 are similar to the previous year's model, but with a slightly different shape. This model design did not sell as well as the 1969 model.

Toploader 4-speed manual transmission. Air conditioning was not available, because there wasn't any space after the engine was installed. After all, this was an ultra-high-performance car and creature comforts were not the priority.

Below are the main differences between the two body styles and changes by year starting with 1969. Two engines were available; early on was the 820S (with hydraulic camshaft) and later in the model year the 820T (with mechanical camshaft.) The car was standard with a seven-blade fan assembly, the large-style wheel hubcaps, but no engine rev limiter. A large rear sway bar and links were mounted under the rear axle and the exhaust was a transverse muffler system with dual intermediate pipes and resonators. On the outside, the huge hood scoop was painted the same color as the car. The inside featured the Deluxe Mach 1 black interior, which was a quality weave.

For 1969, the Boss 429 was offered in five exterior colors:
Raven Black, [A]
Royal Maroon, [B]
Candy Apple Red, [T]
Wimbledon White, [M]
Black Jade, [C]
Interior Trim Code: DAA Black

The Mustang changed very little for 1970. The four headlights dropped to two with air vents on the outside edge of each light. This was a much cleaner design, but not as popular with the collectors; consequently, the earlier cars bring more money at auction than the 1970 model year cars.

In 1970, 499 Boss 429s were produced. The last car was serial number KK NASCAR 2258.

There were five new exterior colors:

Grabber Blue [J]
Grabber Green [Z]
Grabber Orange [U]
Calypso Coral [1]
Pastel Blue [N]

Interior Trim Codes: TA Black & TW White

The hood scoops for this year were painted matte black regardless of the color of the car.

The only transmission available was the Ford Toploader. Air conditioning was not available, again due to space limitations. The Hurst Shifter was available. The new dual inline mufflers were standard.

Here is the breakdown for 1970: Two engines were available: the 820 T and 820 A, both with mechanical camshafts. Aluminum valvecovers were the standard for all engines, and the five-blade flex fan assembly was used to aid in cooling.

Due to the number of damaged engines in 1969, an Autolite engine rev limiter was standard equipment on all 1970 Boss 429 cars.

The smaller Boss 302–type wheel hubcaps became the standard, as did the racing black–painted hood scoop, regardless of the color of the car.

Type Series	Ford Production Automobile
Manufacture and assembly location	Brighton, Michigan, USA
Total production	1,358
Retail price	$4,740
Engine	cast-iron V-8 with aluminum heads
Valvetrain	OHV
Engine displacement	7,030 cc/429.0 ci
Block bore	110.74 mm/4.36 inches
Block stroke	91.2 mm/3.59 inches
Engine compression	10.5
Power output	279.6 kw/374.9 bhp @ 5,200 rpm
Specific power output	53.33 bhp per liter
Bhp/weight	234.17 bhp per ton
Torque	610.12 nm/450.0 ft-lbs @ 3,400 rpm
Transmission	4-speed manual
Gear ratios	2.32:1, 1.69:1, 1.29:1, 1.00:1
Differential	9-inch with nodular-case 3.9 Traction-Loc
Body	unibody with steel
Two-wheel	rear-wheel drive
Wheels	Magnum 500 with chrome rims
Front and rear wheel size	F 38.1 x 17.8 cm/15.0 x 7.0 in
Front and rear tires	F60 x 15 Goodyear RWL Polyglas GT
Rear tires	F60 x 15 Goodyear RWL Polyglas GT
Front brakes	discs with power assist
Rear brakes	drums with power assist
Steering	recirculating ball with power assist
Curb weight	1,601 kg/3,530 pounds
Wheelbase	2,743 mm/108.0 inches
Front and rear track	1,511 mm/59.5 in
Length	4,760 mm/187.4 inches
Width	1,824 mm/71.8 inches
Height	1,280 mm/50.4 inches